SENTENCED
to
'Beyond the Seas'

SENTENCED
to
'Beyond the Seas'

David Clark

GSP

Sentenced to 'Beyond the Seas'
David Clark

Published by Greyhound Self-Publishing 2013
Malvern, Worcestershire, United Kingdom.

Printed and bound by Aspect Design
89 Newtown Road, Malvern, Worcs. WR14 1PD
United Kingdom
Tel: 01684 561567
E-mail: allan@aspect-design.net
Website: www.aspect-design.net

Cover design by David Clark
ISBN 978-1-909219-10-6

CONTENTS

FOREWORD

They say that we all have within us the potential to write a book and I always imagined that my genre would be spies, espionage – something to grip the reader – but I always dismissed it as a momentary fantasy as I lacked the imagination. Little did I realise that something quite different would emerge quite naturally.

In the year 2000 I was deputy mayor of Worcester and preparing for the year to come. One evening while exploring the Guildhall to familiarise myself with everything that I had taken for granted in my previous eleven years as a councillor, I happened to be looking for some regalia that I hadn't seen for some time. The search took me down below the main building which was used to store old broken furniture and packing cases under a mountain of dust.

The area was cold and dark, the ceilings vaulted and the corridors very narrow. I suddenly became acutely aware that I was in the bowels of a very old building actually dating back to 1751. This particular corridor was long with an unexplained gap halfway along to the end where three chambers were situated. Just inside the entrance was a tiny alcove no bigger than a guard's sentry box. This whole configuration was completely different to the cellars I had searched at the other end of the building. So what was the original purpose of this section of the Guildhall?

I mentioned all this to a senior member of staff who had worked there for a great number of years. He explained that I had actually been in the original cells where prisoners were brought from the Worcester gaols waiting to appear in the criminal court sessions which were held in the Guildhall courtroom immediately above. The unexplained gap in the narrow corridor was where an extremely steep staircase had led up into the dock which was situated in the centre of the courtroom, and the alcove area just inside the entrance was probably for the gaoler.

I found this absolutely fascinating and couldn't understand why this little gem hadn't been used to promote more interest in the Guildhall and the history of Worcester. Surely this would be of interest to the many tourists that visited the building?

It was around this time that I came across a 'Rags to Riches' article written in 1985 by Michael Grundy of the then *Worcester Evening News* about a woman called Ann Inett, the unmarried mother of two young children who had been sentenced to death in the Guildhall courtroom. Her sentence had been commuted to transportation to New South Wales where she had served her time, spent a fruitful life and eventually returned as a relatively wealthy woman many years later.

My imagination was well and truly fired by now. I had been standing in the very cell where Ann would have been back in 1786, waiting to appear in court where her very life would be on the line.

I needed to know more about this poor individual and as I researched further, I came across more women who had suffered similar fates. Seven more women emerged: Sarah Davies, Olivia Gascoigne, Mary Abel, Mary Turner, Sarah Bellamy, Mary Cooper and Susannah Hufnell had all been incarcerated in the City or County Gaols, been kept in the Guildhall cells while awaiting their turn in the courtroom above, then back to their gaol to await transportation to 'Terra Australis' the 'Land Beyond the Seas' when they would all join the First Fleet and be part of the birth of a nation.

That was it. I was now on a mission which, although it took nearly a year to accomplish due to lack of resources, ended in the opening up of the cells to the public. I am pleased to say that the response from the public was marvellous and the cells are as popular today as they were back in 2001.

For me though, that was just the beginning. I had to know more of what brought those women to the cells. What did they have to endure? But more importantly – what happened to them afterwards?

So this is how my book emerged as I wanted others to share my intrigue. Not just that though. As the story emerged I kept discovering uncanny coincidences connecting my own life with those of Ann Inett that made this book a consuming passion.

As chairman of licensing for many years I have sat, with my colleagues, in that same courtroom to listen to hearings and offer a judgement on licensing matters such as violations of the licensing laws and infringements of the traffic regulations by taxi drivers. Naturally transportation 'Beyond the Seas' was never an option for those who had offended – even if the thought might have crossed the minds of some councillors!

I lived in Australia back in the sixties and have Australian Citizenship. Little did I know that places where I had lived and worked would be leaping off the pages because of their connection with these women over two hundred and fifty years ago.

Now I would like to share with you what I have learned of these eight Worcester women, some of whom became very successful and respected, one of whom was the progenitor of what was to become the largest family tree that exists in Australia today.

So come on that journey of discovery with me. I sincerely hope that you enjoy reading this little book as much as I did in writing it.

David Clark

I
EIGHT UNFORTUNATE WOMEN

This is a remarkably harsh and uncompromising, yet often inspiring story of eight Worcester area women who were all separately convicted in the courtroom at the city's Guildhall of what, by modern standards, were comparatively petty crimes. Three were sentenced to death by hanging but escaped the gallows, being reprieved and ordered instead to be transported 'beyond the seas' (the term often used in the courts) for seven years or more.

The convicts of this first fleet endured dreadful deprivations in English gaols and aboard the prison ship voyage to New South Wales, but mainly went on to live productive and, some would say, nation-building lives in the new colonies at the other end of the world. Amazingly, six of the Worcester women would also spend time in the tiny new colony on the remote Norfolk Island.

First, you need to know more about these women and what brought them to be the subjects of this book. Strange isn't it – what would they think if they knew that someone, nearly two hundred and fifty years later, would be writing about them?

The first to go through the cells and courtroom of the Worcester Guildhall was Sarah Davies aged twenty-four from Swinford. She appeared at the Worcester Assizes on a charge of theft from the shop of Samuel Mockridge. Her occupation listed as glove maker which was the main industry in Worcester, reaching its peak between 1790 and 1820 when nearly all of the country's supply of gloves came from the local manufacturers. On 2 August 1783 Sarah was sentenced to death for stealing silk handkerchiefs to the value of sixteen shillings.

At the affizes for this county Thos. Wardle was
found guilty of the wilful murder, in March last,
of Mr. Webb, a farmer in the parish of Northfield, by beating out his brains with a large stick,
and afterwards throwing the body into a marl-
pit, on his return from Birmingham market. Immediately after his conviction the judge, in a
most awful and pathetic speech passed sentence
upon him to be executed this day, and his body
to be hung in chains on the further part of
Bromsgrove Lickey, near Northfield. Wardle
during the whole of his trial, and when taken
from the bar, appeared totally unconcerned at
his approaching fate. His lordship gave strict
orders to the gaoler to permit no person to visit
him, except the clergyman and his relations.---
The following also received sentence of death :
Thos. Hartland, John Williams, and John Tim-
mins, for sheepstealing ; Sarah Davies, for shoplifting; John Sincox, for horsestealing ; and John
Harrison, for housebreaking. Hartland is left
for execution, the rest are reprieved.---Edward
Henley, Tho. Collins, Tho. Ratcliff, and Philip Davis, for divers thefts, ordered to be transported to America for seven years. Eliz. Gil-
berts, for receiving stolen goods, fined 10l. and
imprisoned one year ; Tho. Davis, alias Smith,
to be publicly whipped ; seven were acquitted,
and seven discharged by proclamation. Three
being ill ordered to remain till next assizes ; and
seven to remain according to their respective
sentences at former assizes and sessions.

The *Berrow's Worcester Journal* report on the court
proceedings concerning Sarah Davies's case.

Sarah Davies' death sentence for shoplifting was listed amongst several other felons sentenced for murder, sheep and horse stealing. The murderer's case so incensed the judge that he ordered the man to be hung that very day. Fortunately, the judge's wrath did not extend to the others as Sarah's sentence was commuted to transportation to America for seven years, four others were also reprieved to the same fate, one other was to be sent to prison for a year, one was to be whipped, seven were acquitted and seven others freed by proclamation – and all this happening before lunch!

As you will read later, times were hard in those days but Sarah would have been one of the more fortunate ones in having a trade. So why did she have to steal? Although her trade was listed, is it possible that she may have lost her job? That might explain why she found herself in such a dire situation.

Although the report in *Berrow's Worcester Journal* excluded Sarah from the list for transportation, that was indeed to be her fate. She would, however, have to endure a further three years and four months in the Worcester county gaol before being taken by wagon to one of the Southwark Gaols outside London to await embarkation on the ship that would take her, not to America as was the main destination at that time, but to the end of the earth, the new land that would become Australia.

Three women then followed together on 5 March 1785. Mary Abel (spelling of her name varies), a thirty-year-old servant from Hanbury Parish had been charged as follows:

> That Mary Abell otherwise Tilley late of the parish of Hanbury in the county of Worcester on the twelfth day of February . . . with force and arms in the parish aforesaid feloniously did steal take and carry away one Cotton Gown of the value of 3*s* one linen shift of the value of 18*d* and three ells of Hempen cloth of the value of 4*s* 6*d* of the goods and chattels of Robert Wright.

She had a second indictment:

> That Mary Abell feloniously did steal take and carry
> away . . . one linen table cloth of the value of 3s one silk cloak
> of the value of 7s one Camblett Safe Guard of the value of 3s
> one muslin apron of the value of 4s one flaxen apron of the
> value of 18d one Muslin Cap of the value of 1s and one flaxen
> Towel of the value of 1s of the goods and chattels of John Page.

Mary Abell's conduct was clearly not a one off indiscretion as she was convicted of Grand Larceny on no less than four separate indictments. In view of that, she was lucky to be sentenced to seven years transportation rather than receiving the death sentence.

Her alias 'Tilley' is very interesting and presents quite a mystery. How and why did she come to use that name as an alias in 1785? It is a mystery because she would eventually marry a Thomas Tilley on 4 May 1788, not long after their arrival in New South Wales? More on that later.

With her was Mary Turner another servant aged twenty years, a nineteen-year-old servant from the Parish of Holy Cross in Pershore, she was accused of:

> Feloniously stealing one silk cloak value 10s, one pair of
> stays value 16s, one muslin handkerchief value 6s, one lace
> handkerchief value 5s, one muslin apron value 10d, one silk
> handkerchief value 3s, one piece of riband value 2d, and one
> pair of linen gloves value 1s. Goods of Nancy Collins in the
> dwelling house of Thomas Collins on 1 October 24 Geo 3 at
> the parish of Holy Cross.

Mary Turner was convicted and sentenced to seven years transportation.

The other woman that day was the twenty-one-year-old Olivia Gascoigne. Now Olivia is by far the most interesting of our eight women for two reasons. First because of the wealth of speculation about who she really was, second because of the size of the family tree of which she would be the matriarch. Olivia was listed as a servant and sentenced to death together with Edward Hooper and William Lane, for robbery to the value of 227 shillings from the home of her employer George Griffith in August 1784. George Griffith lived at what is now called Moles Cottage in Severn Stoke, a National Heritage listed building.

Olivia's trial was held at the Assizes on 5 March 1785. That Saturday

Mole Cottage, Severn Stoke

Olivia was the second of the prisoners listed on the trial docket to climb up the steep stairs leading from the cells to the dock to face the judge and jury in a crowded court room.

Edward Griffith, son of George Griffith, a farmer in Severn Stoke, was the accuser in Olivia's trial. His indictment was read and accepted by the jury and the foreman read the verdict:

> Worcestershire the Jurors for Lord the King present that Olive Gascoigne spinster late of the parish of Severn Stoke in the County of Worcester on the 10th day of August in the twenty-

fourth year of the reign of our Sovereign Lord George the Third King & with force of Arms at the parish aforesaid in the County aforesaid feloniously did steal take and carry away thirteen pieces of Gold coin of the proper coin of this Realm called Guineas of the value of thirteen pounds and thirteen

Tythe apportionment map of Severn Stoke, 1. shows the site of the Griffith's house.

shillings one piece of foreign Silver Coin called a Dollar of the value of four shillings and sixpence of the Goods Chattels and Money of Edward Griffith in the Dwelling House of George Griffith then and there being found against the peace of our said Lord the King his Crown and Dignity. 'Guilty to be hanged no goods.

At the end of the Assizes, and before he left town, the presiding judge, His Honour George Nares, who was retiring from a life of legal service, requested His Majesty's clemency to commute her sentence (together with others to seven years transportation as his final act from the Bench.

It seems, at first, strange that Edward Griffith should have been the accuser at the trial instead of his father from whom Olivia had stolen. The truth was actually tragic beyond belief. Either that winter must have been particularly harsh or the family suffered a virulent and highly contagious illness because Edward's seventy-three-year-old father George Griffith, his mother, his twenty-year-old nephew John Steight, and his two nieces, Harriet aged nineteen, and Mary aged fifteen, all passed away and were buried in the church cemetery of St Denys in Severn Stoke.

Whilst, at face value, each of these unfortunate female convicts seems to have come from a similar background and class, there has been an element of doubt about Olivia Gascoigne. Not only would her future life prove most eventful, but interest in her early life has produced a swell of highly speculative possibilities that took a lot of research to either verify or discard. I have attempted to cover those speculations in the final chapter of this book. Be that as it may Olivia, whatever her background, would now languish in the county gaol for some sixteen months with Mary Abel and Mary Turner before moving on to a London gaol. Surely they would become quite close over that period, knowing that they all shared the same fate.

Sarah Bellamy would be the next to follow on 9 July 1785. Sarah was born into a very poor family who resided in a double fronted cottage at Queens Hill Belbroughton. She was the sixth child of Richard and Elizabeth Bellamy who would eventually increase their number of children to eight, five girls and three boys.

The Poor Law of 1601 empowered the parishes to levy a tax on all householders which was then administered by overseers appointed by local Justices of the Peace. It was the job of the overseers to use these funds to administer to the poor, needy and infirm of the parish.

James Spurrier was one such overseer. It was he who administered

Tuesday evening ended the assizes for this
county; when John Strickland, for uttering as
true a false bill of exchange for ten pounds,
with intent to defraud Francis Walker and
Elizabeth Collins, was capitally convicted, and
received sentence of death. He is left for execution.——The following also were capitally
convicted, and received sentence of death, but
repriered before the Judge left the town, viz
Edward Hooper, for stealing cloth out of a
warehouse at Upton-upon-Severn; Olive Gaf-
coigne, for stealing out of a box at Severn
Stoke, 19 guineas; Wm. Lane, for stealing
meat, and sundry other things, out of a dwelling house in the night time; and Arthur Ker-
rod, for stealing cloth out of Mr. Mogridge's shop
of this city.——Thomas Morris, for stealing a box
from Mrs Harris's waggon, to be transported for
seven years; as were Mary Turner, for stealing
wearing apparel; and Mary Tilley, alias Abell,
for stealing a cloak and several other things;
Esther Fincher, for stealing a looking-glass from
Mr. Maddocks, imprisoned six months, and to
be whipped; and Sarah Williams, for stealing
seven yards of cotton, out of Mr. Lingham's
shop, imprisoned six months.—Joseph Pretty
removed from Warwick, acquitted of forgery,
but detained on receiving goods under false
pretences.

The *Berrow's Worcester Journal* report of Olivia's trial.

their cottage and he was also responsible for the Bellamy family. It is possible that, due to its size, he used the property on Queens Hill to house several of his charges in order to save on individual payments. It was also common for overseers to arrange employment for children of the poor. Research by the Belbroughton Historical Society reveals that Sarah, at just nine years of age, became apprenticed to Spurrier who was a farmer and a man of some standing in the parish. He farmed at Malthouse Farm just a mile and a half from Queens Hill.

I have visited this property and received a very warm welcome

Spurrier's cottages at Queen's Hill, Belbroughton.

from the owners. Whilst the house looks impressive and large from the front (which it undoubtedly is), the building is surprisingly quite limited in depth. Nevertheless, it is incredibly endowed with age and atmosphere with exposed beams everywhere. I could easily imagine Sarah to have been in those rooms, tending the fire, cleaning, or doing whatever chores she was charged to do.

However, for whatever reason, Sarah did not stay in that

apprenticeship as she is recorded to have been in the employ of the
weaver Benjamin Haden in service to him and his wife Sarah at his
house in Dudley. She couldn't have been there very long as, at the
tender age of fifteen, she was charged with theft:

25th Geo. 3rd 1785

The farm at Belbroughton where Sarah was in service, now known as Bell End Farm.

Benj. Haden. One promissory note signed under the hand of
Wm Jackson for the gover[nor] and co. of Bank of Eng[land]
No. 6010 bearing date 11th April 1785 val[ue] £10. One other
Promis[sory] note signed under the hand of Thoms Hill Junr
for Hill Waldron bears date 2nd May 1785 whereby the sd Thos
Hill did for the sd Hill Waldron and Co promise to pay the
bearer 5 guineas on demand at Sir Jas Esdaile Hamnett and
Esdaile Bankers London val. recd £5 and 5s of the said notes
at the time of commit[ing] the felony afsd [aforesaid] being
the property of Benj Haden and the sd promis[sory] £10 and
£5 5s respectively payable and secured by the sd promis[sory]
notes respectively being then due and unsatisfied to the sd
Benj Haden the property thereof at pish [parish] of Dudley
29th May 25th G 3rd [25th year of George III].

Sarah was tried at Worcester on July 9 1785 before Judge Baron Horlam with Benjamin and Sarah Haden appearing as witnesses for the prosecution. However, this whole event was more involved than first appeared because Benjamin Haden was experiencing severe financial difficulties and was due to face a charge of bankruptcy at the Summer Assizes. Is it possible that his own evidence against Sarah could have been coloured or exaggerated in order to mitigate his own problem?

Was he forced into bankruptcy because of his financial loss caused by the theft? Or was the charge against Sarah fabricated in

Berrow's Worcester Journal report of 14 July 1785:

order to cover up his financial situation? There is some doubt in all this as there was no mention at all of the promissory notes at his bankruptcy hearing.

In any event, Sarah was found guilty of Grand Larceny and Judge Horlam pronounced sentence, 'to be transported beyond the seas for The term of seven years'. It was then recorded that Sarah, 'guiltily prayed to be publicly whipp'd at afternoon of the next two market days'. She pleaded in vain and the sentence stood.

There is a question here as to why she was only sentenced to seven years when the sum involved was so large and would normally have incurred the death penalty? Was it because of her tender age? Or could it be that the 'value' of the theft was dubious? It was certainly not unknown for the value of goods to be exaggerated either for revenge and to secure as strong a sentence as possible, or for the victim of theft in some way to absolve themselves of the greater debt. Was that the case here? Coincidentally, Sarah's trial took place on the very day Ann Inett was committing her crime.

Two weeks later on 19 July 1785, Mary Cooper a thirty-six-year-old charwoman, would receive the same sentence for stealing clothing of unknown value (petite larceny). Her crime was committed within the city. As a consequence she would have been committed to the city gaol which was situated in Friar Street at that time.

Ann Inett would follow nearly one year later on 11 March 1786. Ann, aged twenty-eight, was listed as a mantua maker when she was sentenced to death for the theft of various items of clothing to the value of twenty shillings. Thanks to the research done by her descendant Edward Inett, we know quite a lot about Ann. She was born at Abberley in 1754, the youngest of four children of Samuel and Mary Inett. Her father had died when she was barely three years of age. As a young woman, she made her living from dressmaking and had two illegitimate children – Thomas, born in 1778 when she was aged twenty-four, and Constance born in 1781 when she was twenty-seven. Both were christened at Bayton Church near Rock.

Then came the events of 1785 and 1786 when, for some unknown reason, she was driven into crime. *Berrow's Worcester Journal* of 14 July 1785 first reported, 'The dwelling-house of Susannah Brookes in Grimley has been broken open and several articles of her wearing apparel taken thereout.'

The same edition also carried a public notice offering a reward to anyone giving information leading to the conviction of the house-breaker involved. The following week's *Berrow's Worcester Journal* was able to report that Ann Inett, late of the Parish of Grimley, had been apprehended for the crime and taken into custody. She had been arrested by Mr Jones, who was possibly the official of the court, otherwise known as the Constable – not to be confused with the police constables of today.

She had been apprehended on suspicion of robbing the house of Susan Brookes of Grimley. Some of the property was found on her, the rest in her lodgings. She had stolen one linen gown, one plaid petticoat, one sewn handkerchief, one gauze cap with straw coloured ribbon, I muslin apron, one muslin handkerchief, one black hood, three stockings, one round cap, two ribbons and a striped muslin flounced apron. Her trial is covered more fully later.

Finally on 2 October 1786 came Susannah Hufnell, yet another

> At the quarter Seffions of this city on Monday laft, Sufannah Huffnell was convicted of ftealing three, and ordered for transportation; alfo Mary Cooper, for ftealing a gown, received a fimilar fentence; —— Williams, for ftealing horfe-fhoes, was ordered to be publickly whipped; and —— M'Cabe, for ftealing table linen, was ordered private punithment.—The fentence of Huffnell and Cooper gives general fatisfaction, by ridding the county of two very dangerous and abandoned characters.

servant aged twenty-two accused of stealing clothing within the city, and sentenced to seven years transportation. Her incarceration in Worcester gaol, where she would meet Mary Cooper, would last only three weeks before being transferred to a Southwark gaol.

So, those are our female felons and the reasons why they found themselves going through the cells and court room of the Guildhall.

Having introduced our subjects, we need to recognise the world and times in which they lived – their surroundings, the stresses and strains of surviving in those times.

II
THE WORCESTER GAOLS

Worcester had two gaols at that time. The city gaol which served just the city and the county gaol which was situated within the old castle. The County Gaol, built about 1653, was the larger of the two prisons and was a strong building of brick and stone and had been built within the castle precincts to serve as a House of Correction for the county. The castle itself was situated close to the motte by the river and adjacent to the cathedral.

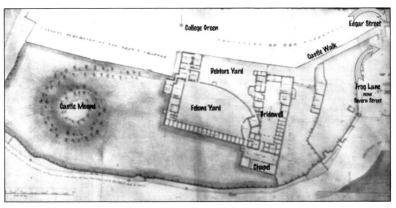

Plan of the county gaol *c.*1722.

The entrance was by way of the lane (now known as Castle Place) just south of the Edgar Tower by Worcester Cathedral and lay close to the river. This site is now occupied by Kings School buildings to the south of College Green.

Being over one hundred and thirty years old the gaol was no longer at its best. Just three years earlier, in 1783, it had suffered a virulent attack of gaol fever, and in 1788 it was visited and condemned by John Howard, the great prison reformer. Prisons were run on a quite different basis from those of today. They were often run by a local person, for the profit of that person, so any considerations for the prisoner's health or comfort would have been absolutely minimal. It is believed that at one time this gaol was run by the local butcher.

The gaol was one of the regular attractions of the city, for on Assize Sunday (the Sunday during or immediately following the Assize) prisoners were shown to the crowds, It was often a rowdy affair with spectators paying six pence to the gaoler for pointing out those condemned to be executed before the procession would proceed to the gallows on Red Hill. It was not uncommon for prisoners going to their execution to be already dressed in a shroud and with their coffin in the same cart.

The city gaol was completely different. This facility only held prisoners taken within the city walls and was situated in Friar Street immediately adjacent to one of Worcester's most iconic historic houses now know as Greyfriars. It is difficult for us today to fully realise what this prison was really like. It was, in fact, a converted house. The authorities had purchased the building from the clothier William Goldwyne in 1724 and changed its use to the gaol and house of correction. Goldwyne had then leased it back to run it as a private concern. An astute financial move, I would have thought.

Years later a purpose built gaol would be erected and would then end up purchased and demolished by William Laslett in 1828 in order to erect almshouses for the poor of the parish.

The plans of the old city gaol are illustrated and show its situation opening on to Friar Street. The two areas for the prisoners lie immediately either side of the entrance passage which leads through to the felon's yard. The jailer's quarters can be seen either side of the second passage which then opens out into the debtor's yard. A third small yard at the rear of the property is reserved for the female prisoners.

How secure could this gaol have been?

Friar Street as it used to be.

Friar Street as it is today. The city gaol was situated just beyond
Greyfriars, the large building in the centre of this picture.

Today's street scene opposite the site of the old city gaol which would have been on the right of this photo.

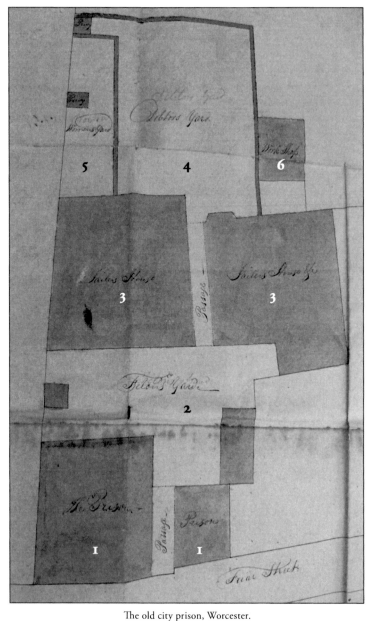

The old city prison, Worcester.
1. prison, 2. felon's yard, 3.jailer's house, 4. debtor's yard, 5. women's yard, 6. workshop.

III
ENGLAND AROUND 1780

To better understand why these women might have ended up on the wrong arm of the law it might help to realise the world they lived in.

George III was on the throne, In fact, within two years of the last of our women being sentenced, His Majesty George III would grace the Guildhall with his presence during a visit to the Three Choirs Festival, an event which continues to this day. Reports of a banquet held for him in the Assembly Room note that:

> The most genteel reception of all was that on the morning of 8th August 1788, when King George III, who with Queen Charlotte and three of the princesses were attending the Three Choirs Festival, paid a visit to the Corporation at the Guildhall. He described the Assembly Room 'a handsome gallery' and proposed a toast of 'Prosperity to the City and the Corporation of War'.

As a result, the King presented his portrait to the city to commemorate his visit which still hangs in the assembly room to this day. Lord Nelson, a future freeman of the city of Worcester and the Duke of Wellington were just teenagers with their careers before them.

As for people of the time, this was the century of such notables as: Paul Revere, Benjamin Franklin, Marie Antoinette, Johan Sebastian Bach, Blackbeard the pirate, Samuel Johnson the great diarist, and George Washington who would become president of America.

Beyond our shores, the American Revolution was over culminating in the Declaration of Independence of 1776, the effects of which would have a material effect on our eight women as America had, up until then, been the repository for our unwanted convicts. Nearer to home, events in France were building up to the start of the French Revolution which was to erupt in 1789.

The preceding seventeenth century had experienced enormous change due, in the main, to fundamental differences in faith. First, the English Civil War had resulted in the abolition and then the restitution of the monarchy. Then, towards the end of the century and in the face of fervent catholic opposition, a protestant succession had been created which would prevail for more than the succeeding four hundred years. Then there was the expectation that the 1707 Act of Union between England and Scotland quickly followed in 1713 by the end of the European wars would herald a period of prosperity for the general populace – but, alas, this was not to be so. Britain, as the Union was now known, was bureaucratic, still militarised and heavily taxed (a bit like today!) and the wars of faith between republicans and royalists, Tories and Whigs, colonialists and natives waged across the Union and across Europe, America and India throughout the new century.

Portrait of King George III.

But what about the ordinary English inhabitant who would be totally ignorant of much of these national and international events? Certainly, even if they had been aware, their concerns would have been centred on the issues that affected them directly. Their daily worries were how to provide for their families and how to meet the ever-increasing demands of the local landowners.

It was around this time that a private Act of Parliament brought about the Land Enclosures Act – the confiscation of common land that had, up to then, been cultivated by families for their own provision and meagre income. This Act impacted on local life like no other. Almost half of the population worked on the land. In areas such as Worcester, this proportion would inevitably be higher. This new legislation meant that that those who had clung to their plots where they could eke out a living so long as they also had access to common land where they could graze their sheep and cattle were now reduced to day-wage labourers.

These homesteaders now had to find paid work in order to provide for their families, but where could such work be found when there was precious little available? Some found work in the rural industries – as coopers, farriers and such like but the majority were reduced to finding casual seasonal labour such as ditch-digging and other temporary backbreaking tasks. The result of all this was an increasing migration to the towns with their homes being abandoned to deteriorate causing the desolation and loss of so many of the small hamlets throughout the land. England's population at this time stood at just six and a half million. Life expectancy was barely thirty-seven years, and the average weekly income for a farmer was three shillings from which he would have to pay four pence for a loaf of bread. For those who worked on the land the average weeks work, if available, was eighty hours. For the rural worker it only needed a poor crop and life would suddenly become very hard indeed. That would then knock on to the rest of the community as prices would rise and jobs would be lost.

Consider now what you would do in this position. No work, no money, no welfare system and a family to feed. Your only thoughts would have to be to survival. So perhaps one might be forgiven for stealing that loaf of bread or taking a few potatoes from your neighbour's field. It becomes easy to realise how hard life really was in those sad days, especially in winter. It would be inconceivable today but it was relatively common then for daughters to be sold into prostitution just to obtain bread. Little children were sold into virtual slavery, again just for a few pennies. Normally honest people were, by sheer desperation, driven to steal just to stave off the workhouse or worse, starvation. Certainly the future for so many was bleak indeed.

So crime became rampant as so many had to fight for survival. The courts were full of such miscreants – I can't really call them 'criminals' as their motivation was, in the main, never really dishonourable. But the problem was reaching epidemic proportions and needed a solution in order to protect society in general. Legislators decided that because only a minute proportion of criminals were able to be arrested (there being no real ability to police and detect crime), and because 'crime' was so prevalent – even in order just to live – that they had to wreak a punishment so terrible on those that were convicted so as to deter others from taking up a life of crime. So punishment became harsh indeed – so harsh that it is almost impossible to appreciate today. What could be more of a deterrent than death by hanging? Regrettably this did little to deter those who faced death by starvation anyway – so what had they to lose?

Such was the desperation of so many in those sad times that life became incredibly cheap. People could be hanged for merely stealing just a handkerchief. Children not yet teenagers could suffer the same fate for picking pockets or setting fire to a haystack as one poor young boy did. No-one was immune except for pregnant mothers who would plead 'their belly' with the sentence being delayed only until after the baby was born or the pregnancy found to be a lie.

One big failing in these times was the lack of any kind of police force, not only to maintain law and order, but to investigate offences to be heard by the courts. It would take another forty-five years before the Home Secretary Sir Robert Peel introduced an organised, uniformed police force. The result was that many of the cases brought to court might have been due to an opportunistic person seeking to collect a much needed financial reward which could often be found advertised in the local newspaper in order to apprehend the perpetrator of a crime. By far the majority of criminal cases were brought to court by the victims, who then presented their 'complaint' together with any relevant evidence for the court then to offer a judgement

Invariably the courts then chose between two options – set the defendant free or give a severe punishment – which frequently meant the death sentence. What is very sad is that people's lives were invariably dispensed with the say so of just one person and with little or no investigation. Such was the case with our eight Worcester women.

The list of crimes attracting the death sentence is far too long to be repeated here however, not all of those sentenced to death were actually executed. Probably less than sixty per cent actually suffered the ultimate fate. This was because it became clear to those sitting in judgement that in the late eighteenth century, with over two hundred felonies for which the penalty was death, that the 'Bloody Code' as it was known was simply making life incredibly cheap. However, it took until 1911 before the code was finally abolished.

With so many felons needing to be punished, one of the solutions had been to ship them off to the American colonies never to be seen again. Most of these deportees were sent to Maryland and Virginia, but some ended up in Barbados to work on the sugar plantations. Out of sight, out of mind.

The American War of Independence (1775–83) meant that we no longer held any influence in that part of the world and could no longer use that colony to relieve the pressure on our gaols which were now full to overflowing. Hanging, of course, was one way of dealing with the problem but another needed to be found, so alternatives to the American colonies were investigated.

Some fifteen years previously, in 1770, Captain James Cook had discovered the east coast of New Holland which he named New South Wales. He had sailed the whole of the New South Wales coast and reported to the British government that he thought it would make a good place for a settlement.

Britain did not recognise the country as being inhabited as the Aborigine natives did not cultivate the land, and were, therefore, 'uncivilized'. Such arrogance that would never be tolerated these days.

So, on 18 August 1786, the decision was made to use Cook's New South Wales as the ideal site for a new penal colony.

There was an official list of crimes that were punishable by deportation: all theft above the value of one shilling; receiving stolen goods, jewels and plate; stealing lead, iron, copper, and ore from black lead mines (what about other mines?); stealing from furnished lodgings; stealing letters; stealing fish from a pond or river, stealing roots, trees or plants; stealing a shroud from a grave (why would you do this?); setting fire to underwood; assault with intent to rob; bigamy and clandestine marriage; assaulting, cutting or burning clothes (I suspect this disappointed a few wronged wives who would like to have used this for revenge); counterfeiting the copper coin; watermen carrying too many passengers on the Thames resulting in a passenger drowning; incorrigible rogues who broke out of prison, and persons reprieved from capital punishment; embezuling naval stores.

But – was the sentence of transportation 'beyond the seas' actually

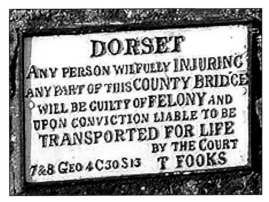

Another offence for which you could be transported.

legal? The authority for questioning the legality of the transportation of convicts comes from Peter McKay's *A Nation Within a Nation,* p. 15.

There is reference to the *Oxford Companion to Law* which states that, 'Warrants of custody have never been valid outside of Britain.'

Enshrined in English law since the act of 1640, but dating back to the reign of Henry II in the twelfth century, by *habeas corpus,* not even a criminal shall be sent prisoner beyond the seas. The first English textbook on law, Coke's *Institutes of the Lawes of England* 1641 states that:

> No subject of this realm that is a resident of the Kingdom of England shall be sent prisoner into ports, garrisons, islands or places resident of the Kingdom of England or places beyond the seas, and that every such imprisonment is hereby enacted and adjudged to be illegal.

Regardless of this however, transportation continued.

So that was how life was around 1785.

IV
THE WORCESTER GUILDHALL

The title of this book is all about the connection between the Guildhall and the new colony, so I want to tell you more about Worcester's principal civic building. The Guildhall is inexorably connected to Terra Australis (Land of the South) due to events that took place between 1783–86 and because this is where the courts of the day were situated.

There has been a Guildhall on this site since 1227 when the citizens of Worcester were granted a charter by Henry III which, among other privileges, permitted the establishment of a guild of merchants to control the trade within the city. Their hall was known as the Guild's Hall and eventually became the centre of administration for the city as well as the local Court of Justice. Despite subsequent rebuilding and the demise of the guild of merchants, the original name was retained and Worcester's town hall continues to be known as the Guildhall.

The original building was a timber-framed structure with a rather longer high street frontage than now, but occupied the same site. The area in front was constructed as a square containing a row of shops. The hall itself contained the Courts of Justice, one at each end with the prison to the north; this included a notorious dungeon called the peep-hole. Close by, adjoining the gaoler's house, was an alehouse from which the gaoler sold very expensive beer to such of the prisoners as could afford it. In addition to its judicial use, plays were acted in the hall and it was even used for the game of tennis. Perhaps this was the reason why all citizens who became members of the Corporation had their fees increased by sixteen shillings and eight pence 'towards the glass windows'.

The Guildhall was a very old building by the early 1700s bearing in mind it had also undoubtedly suffered from the ravages of the Civil War that had begun and ended at Worcester (1642–51). Tradition has it that it was in this part of the High Street that the Royalists made their last stand. Bodies of soldiers wounded in battle were brought into the building and it is recorded that it required extensive disinfecting as a result of the blood, gore and severed limbs – the aftermath of war.

The Guildhall today

In those days, a city taken by storm could expect little mercy and the Parliamentarians were in a mood of grim vengeance. One of the sources of restraint and clemency was Edward Elvins, Oliver Cromwell's choice of military governor who had been mayor of Worcester 1646–47.

The decision to rebuild the ancient Guildhall was taken in March 1717 but, probably due to financial difficulties, work was not begun until 1721. The main central block of the Guildhall was completed

The leather fire buckets on the south wall.

The north end of the Assembly Room which King George III found 'handsome'.

in 1724 and has changed little since then. The statue above the main entrance is that of Queen Anne and those either side are of Charles I (holding a church) and Charles II (with orb and sceptre). The five figures on the parapet represent (from left to right) Hercules (Labour), Peace, Justice, Plenty and Chastisement.

The two wings of the building were originally completely self-contained and were built slightly later – the north wing in 1725 and the south wing in 1727. The south wing was used as the judge's lodging during the Assizes until 1835 when the county courts moved to the newly erected Shirehall in Foregate Street. Later it would be used as a coffee house.

The new Guildhall must have been crowded and bustling like its predecessor. Space was required for the courts, cells, assembly rooms as well as more common municipal activities.

On the south wall, still there for the visitor to see are the leather fire buckets awaiting the toll of St Andrews church bells – the city's fire alarm. The buckets were paid for by the Corporation but no arrangement made for any fire-fighters. In 1769 they put out a large fire in Mealcheapen Street but only after having to ply a group of soldiers with copious quantities of ale. The building was well suited for its judicial civic and social functions. The lower hall had two courts towards the back of the building with two rooms, one for tea and the other for cards. On the top floor was the Council Chamber, later known as the Assembly Room favoured so much by George III.

As already mentioned, the Guildhall contained two courts – one civil (the *nisi prius*), the other criminal. Interestingly, the main entrance to the hall was constructed wide enough for two judges to enter side-by-side, meaning that neither one would have to defer to the other in terms of importance or seniority. They could enter on equal terms before veering off, one going left for the civil court, part of which is now the Mayor's Parlour, and the other right to the criminal court with its tiny staircase from the cells below once opening out in the dock in the centre of the room.

The court room suffered a terrible accident just thirty-seven years after the completion of the new building. It happened during one of the city Assize Courts when a sudden storm blew down a cluster of chimneys which crashed through the roof killing six people immediately, mortally injuring others and leaving dozens more seriously hurt. Sir Eardley Wilmott, judge of the King's Bench, who was presiding at the time, wrote to his wife, 'The roof beat down upon us . . . I escaped without the least hurt . . . although I despaired of my life . . . Mr John Lawes is killed and the attorney in the case I was trying is killed.'

To this day, the top of the arch in the main wall contains the latin motto, *Fiat justitia ruat coelum* (let justice be done though the heavens fall).

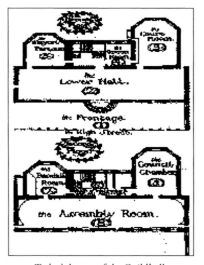

Today's layout of the Guildhall.

Not that the convicts who went through that room would have had any idea of what it meant, even if they might well have prayed for such an incident to save them.

These days the court room retains its name and is used for all kinds of meetings but still retains its judicial heritage as most Licensing hearings are held there. The dock and divisions for the various officials however, have gone.

These courts were originally open to the lower hall and visitors can see the arches of the courts on the facing walls as they enter. However, such was the sheer noise of proceedings that the openings to the Lower Hall had to be walled up with doorways in order for a degree of privacy. One can only imagine the commotion when a brief trial culminated in the grim and distressing sentence of death being handed down to so many unfortunates for crimes that today would probably warrant a little more than a ticking off.

Children too were dealt with harshly – mostly in the civil court. They were certainly not beyond the ultimate sentence. A more than

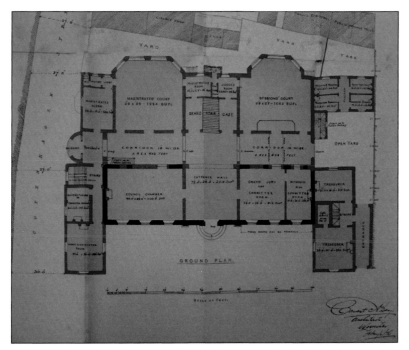

No plans exist for the original layout of the Guildhall. But this plan, dated 1876, which was never adopted, shows the two courts with partial walling-in of the arches.

frequent punishment would be a flogging that was carried out in the Yard behind the Guildhall. However, such was the distress caused to those living in close proximity by the desperate shrieks and wailing of these poor children that it was thought best that the floggings should take place inside and below the building in order to suppress the sounds and put a stop to the complaints.

Also below the Guildhall are vaulted cellars, used today for storage, that stretch from below the south wing along the length of the Guildhall to the kitchen area which then abuts the cell section.

Access to the cells is by way of a door down a few steps to the rear of the building, along a very narrow, thirty-foot corridor, which then opens on to two small cells, and one larger one. Even today it is quite cold down there, so imagine what it would have been like two hundred and fifty years ago with no sanitation, lack of air and

The entrance to the court room with its archway, now enclosed.

numerous unwashed people crammed together awaiting their few moments in the court room above. When the call came, they would be escorted back along the corridor to an opening on the left which offered an extremely steep and narrow staircase to bring them up into the dock in the centre of the court. They would then see that they were surrounded by the judge, prosecution, defence (if they were lucky), court officials and a morbidly expectant audience.

The court proceedings of the day were reported in *Berrow's Worcester Journal*, the world's oldest surviving newspaper still in circulation to this day.

The entrance to the cells at the rear of the Guildhall and below the court room (above left).
The long corridor to the cells (above right).
The marks on the wall indicate the steepness of the old stairway to the court above (below).

How the court room used to appear.

The court room as it is today.

A 1786 edition of *Berrow's Worcester Journal*.

V
SENTENCED TO DEATH

The first of our unfortunate women was Sarah Davies. On the morning of 2 August 1783 she would have been taken from her cell next to the Bridewell of the county gaol within the old castle and transported by cart to the Guildhall with other prisoners due to have their cases dealt with that day.

The route would most likely have proceeded from the Old Castle through the Edgar Tower into Edgar Street and then left into Sidbury. At this point it might possibly have continued into Friers Street (now Friar Street) to pick up more miscreants from the City Gaol, or it would have gone down Leech Street past the Lych Gate and into the High Street. The cart would then turn left into Cooken Street (now Copenhagen Street) then right into the rear yard of the Guildhall to the entrance to the cells below the courtroom.

So, on that August morning, Sarah and the other miserable prisoners might have 'enjoyed' some fresh air, away from the smell of the cells, while being taken by cart on the short journey to the rear of the Guildhall.

Sarah with the other prisoners in turn would have been marshalled round the back of the building down the steps and through the small door, along the narrow stone-walled passageway into the three cells immediately below the court to await the bailiff's calling. Despite whatever weather prevailed outside, you can be sure that the atmosphere down in those cells would have been dark, cold and uninviting.

Fear would have been in their minds and despair in their hearts. The walk from those miserable cells to the courtroom was a short

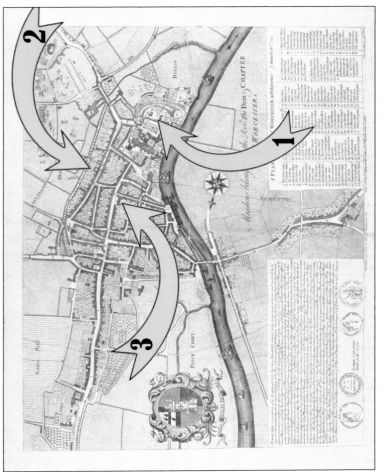

Map showing the county gaol (1.) the city gaol (2.) and the Guildhall (3.)

one. Halfway along the narrow, thirty-foot corridor, they would ascend the exceedingly steep staircase to appear in the centre of the court above.

The courts were rowdy affairs in those days with enthusiastic participation from the morbidly interested audience. This, together with the imposing presence of the judge in his robes and wig, the officials of the court and the prosecuting barrister must have been enough to strike fear in anyone finding themselves in the dock.

Sarah, having been sentenced to death, would later have her sentence commuted to seven years transportation to the American colonies. However, the War of Independence had brought that destination to an end so she would languish in the county gaol for over three years while the government came up with an alternative. While she would no doubt have seen many convicts pass through the gaol, it would be eighteen months before she would meet the next of her eventual colleagues.

Olivia Gascoigne, Mary Turner and Mary Abel would be the next to go through that same court process all on the same day. These three will have all shared the same exercise yard at the county gaol so will have been well acquainted and have common fears and anticipation to talk about on the short ride to the Guildhall cells.

Sarah Bellamy, the youngest, would follow four months later to join the 'county gaol set'. Then, two weeks later, Mary Cooper who was a city citizen and would have gone to the city gaol in Friar Street. Her journey to the court would have taken her a short way down Friar Street past John Dovey the carpenter and George Morgan the glover who both had shops within what is now Greyfriars. Then, turning left at the corner shop owned by Thomas Evans the skinner, into Pump Street it would pass the baker's shop run by John Day then John Hooper's cheese shop. As the Quarter Sessions and Assize Courts were quite an occasion, it is possible that the customers of the Horse and Jockey and The Crown public houses might well have taken to the streets to watch the unfortunates go by. I can imagine one person keeping watch for the gaoler's cart in order that the drinkers should not miss the spectacle. Some might even have followed the cart in order to be a spectator at the court proceedings.

Having had her case dealt with, Mary would return to the city gaol where she would spend more than a year before being joined by Susannah Hufnell.

The last two would then be Ann Inett who went to the county gaol and Susannah Hufnell who was incarcerated in the city gaol with Mary Cooper. However, Ann Inett's day in court is worth special mention as it shows the low value put on life. Any fear felt by prisoners would have been well justified on that March morning of Ann's trial in 1786 because all seventeen prisoners that morning, were to receive the death sentence.

That in itself is remarkable, but consider just how long each trial must have taken. How much time was given to the presentation of the case? Then, of course, any evidence that would have to be offered. It is clear that any opportunity to offer some kind of defence must have been extremely limited. It is highly likely that each case could have taken little more than fifteen to twenty minutes. How cheap was life that day!

There are no surviving accounts of Ann's trial save the entry in the following Thursday's *Berrow's Worcester Journal* of 16 March 1786. The entry merely states:

> On Monday, the Assizes were held at our Guildhall, when Ann Inett, for burglary; Michael Gough, for burglary; George Rowley for stopping Thomas Hopkins and Edward Earl on the highway; Thomas Johnson for robbing Mr Jenkins of a pocketbook; Jacob Joseph for stealing the bag containing the Droitwich mail; William Prosser, for robbing and ill-treating William Drinkwater on the highway near this city; James Rogers for robbing Mary Ellins on the highway; Richard Watts for robbing Mr Blizard of Pershore, and others, on the highway; Thomas Neale for breaking open a house at Ombersley; John Smith and Thomas Butler, for sheep-stealing; George Moule, the younger, for horse stealing; Mary Goddard and Elizabeth Richards, for robbing John Sheppey, of a Worcester Bank Bill, two guineas in gold, and some silver; William Baker, for stealing out of a desk at the Star and garter Inn, in this city, six guineas in gold, and other money; William Bailey, for sheep-stealing; and Joseph Cooke, for robbing Mr Saunders of this city, were capitally convicted and received sentence of death.

Chillingly, the *Berrow's Worcester Journal* reported that within days of their sentencing: 'Gough, Johnson, Prosser, Watts, Neale, Moule and Cooke were executed on the gallows at Red-hill.'

WORCESTER.

On Monday the affizes for this city and county were held at our Guildhall, when Ann Junett, for burglary; Michael Gough, for burglary; George Rowley, for

ftopping Thomas Hopkins and Edward Earl on the highway; Thomas Johnfon, for robbing Mr. Jennings of a pocket-book; Jacob Jofeph, for ftealing the bag containing the Droitwich mail; William Proffer, for robbing and ill treating William Drinkwater on the highway near this city; James Rogers, for robbing Mary Ellins, on the highway; Richard Watts, for robbing Mr. Blizard of Perfhore, and others, on the highway; Thomas Neale, for breaking open a houfe at Omberfley; John Smith and Thomas Butler, for fheep-ftealing; George Moule, the younger, for horfe-ftealing; Mary Goddard, and Elizabeth Richards, for robbing John Sheppey, of a Worcefter Bank-bill, two guineas in gold, and fome filver; William Baker, for ftealing out of a defk at the Sar and Garter Inn, in this city, fix guineas in gold, and other money; William Bailey, for fheep-ftealing; and Jofeph Cooke, for robbing Mr. Saunders of this city, were capitally convicted and received fentence of death.

Gough, Johnfon, Proffer, Watts, Neale, Moule, and Cooke, are left for execution, and the others are reprieved.

William Mountford, for attempting to rob John Perkes of Bromfgrove; James Gutteridge, for breaking into a malt-houfe; Samual Harbidge, for theft; John Thomafon, for ftealing linen cloth; and Daniel Colley, were fentenced to be tranfported for feven years; John Winwood, for a rape on the body of Elizabeth Bever, to ftand in the pillory on Saturday

The extract from *Berrow's Worcester Journal*, 16 March 1786.

The report goes on to list five more unfortunates sentenced to seven years transportation, several to prison terms one to stand in the pillory before going to prison for rape and quite a number to be whipped.

At the end of the day's court proceedings the convicts would have been taken back to their respective gaols where they will have sought the solace of their fellow prisoners some of whom were awaiting trial and the rest who were serving their sentences. By the time the last of our women were retuned after court, the longest serving had already been incarcerated for more than three years, and five of them for more than a year.

It is a fair assumption, by our standards today, that the three who had their sentences commuted would have been mightily relieved. But we have to imagine the values of the 1700s. Remember that our women would not be well educated. By our standards they would be simple folk with deep superstitions, probably god-fearing and extremely fearful of the unknown. They were mostly from poor peasant stock who had probably never been more than a few miles away from home in their lives. As for their future, they had never seen the sea and would have no concept of what a ship might be like.

Some contemporary reports indicate that it was not unknown for some who had been sentenced to deportation to plead for the rope as this was deemed less fearsome. Possibly the prospect of meeting their maker was a better choice to being transported to the hell of an unknown land 'beyond the seas'. The following reports from *Berrow's Worcester Journal* gave the populace an idea of what may await all deportees. This one had already appeared earlier in October 1785:

> " On Tuesday 109 convicts, call for transportation, were carryed on board a vessel bound for Abacco, one of the Bahama Islands; where a life of regularity and labour may perhaps reclaim the most of them, from being the pest and outcast of society, to be useful members of the community."

Then a more contemporary update appeared in the 6 November 1786 edition of the paper:

> wright by trade.
>
> It is said, that ships are to proceed annually to Botany Bay with convicts from the several gaols in the kingdom.——Those, who are in the high road to this new settlement, should be reminded, that no ale-houses, no gin-shops are to be found there.——Task-work or carte,—will be the only alternative. Necessity will exact sobriety and industry in that desolate country.——If prudence could but supercede necessity, and teach the practice of industry and sobriety here, many would be rescued from the misery of this long voyage to a country from whence they never can return. It is imagined the ships will be nine months on their passage to Botany Bay.

We don't know how much notice the women would have been given of their pending transportation, but Susannah Hufnell would have only three weeks in gaol after sentencing before she, and Mary Cooper, would set off on their long, and arduous, journey to the Hulk Dunkirk at Plymouth which served as a collection point for prisoners from various gaols as they were assembled for the First Fleet.

> On Tuesday Mary Cooper, and Sussannah Hufnell, re sent off from this city, to Plymouth, previous their embarkation for Botany Bay.

Their journey to Portsmouth would have entailed a ten day trip by ox-wagon built to carry up to eight people with one or two benches crosswise in front and two back seats arranged lengthwise and facing inwards. Besides being individually linked the prisoners would also have been chained to the benches or to the sides of the wagon. They would have been fed at the discretion of their gaoler and slept where their convoy rested overnight until they reached their destination. Remember also, that this was in November, so they would have been desperately cold for the duration of the trip and they would have needed to huddle together in order to combat the weather conditions.

The hulks that awaited these poor women were old merchant and slave ships that had been decommissioned. Converting the ships to prison hulks involved removal of the rigging, masts, rudders, and various other features required for sailing. Some hulks retained some of these features, but all were rendered inoperable or unseaworthy in some way. The internal structure was also reconfigured with various features, including jail cells, in order to accommodate convicted criminals or occasionally prisoners of war.

These hulks, which retained only their ability to float, were typically located in harbours and some were moored on the Thames. This made them convenient temporary holding quarters for convicts awaiting transportation to Australia and other penal colonies within the British Empire. In 1798 the hulks held more than one thousand, four hundred out of about one thousand, nine hundred people awaiting transportation. The hulks, in general, were certainly evil places as they were rat infested, dank, rank smelling, fetid, and disease ridden.

Whilst the county gaols were very undesirable places to be, the

A typical hulk of the time.

hulks must have been ten times worse. Life on board these floating prisons was absolutely appalling. Hygiene was unheard of so disease spread quickly. The sick received scant attention and were not even separated from the healthy.

Just two months after convicts had been placed in shackles on board the first of these hulks, an epidemic of gaol fever (a form of typhus spread by vermin) spread among them. It persisted, on and off, for almost three years. Dysentery, caused by brackish water, was also widespread. At first sufferers, whatever their state, lay on the bare floors. Later they were given straw mattresses and their irons removed. As a result, mortality rates of thirty per cent were common. Between 1776 and 1795, nearly two thousand out of almost six thousand convicts serving their sentence on board hulks died.

So this was what Susannah and Mary would have to endure. In fact, conditions were so bad at one time that the officer in charge complained, 'many of the prisoners are nearly if not quite naked.'

The superintendent of the Dunkirk hulk had written a shocked protest to the authorities on 25 August 1784, which resulted in a Code of Orders being drawn up to protect the women. The women prisoners held on board were often brutalised and used by the marines supposed to be guarding them which inevitably resulted in pregnancy. This partially explains the number of births on the voyage of the First Fleet. There is another explanation for these relationships – a liaison with your gaoler could be a way of securing a more tolerable existence with the benefits of such things as material comforts or the security of protection from such brutality. It was not beyond the realms of possibility that a liaison of this kind might result in a more permanent arrangement which did happen between some prisoners and their guards during the actual voyage.

After their unpleasant stay, thankfully only five months, on the Dunkirk, Susannah and Mary were then embarked on the prison transport ship *Friendship* to await their sailing into the unknown. Four weeks would pass after Susannah and Mary's departure from Worcester before Abel, Bellamy, Turner and Davies would take their similar but shorter journey of six to eight days from Worcester to their next gaol in Southwark which was then situated just outside London.

This would not be such a comfortable journey for Mary Abel because she was some four months pregnant from a liaison with either a gaoler or a convict.

Just one week later they would be joined by Olivia and Ann. Descendants of these two women believe that a firm friendship probably emerged from this journey. Again, apart from the two sent to the Dunkirk, the rest of our women were now together for their voyage to 'Beyond the Seas'.

There were a number of gaols in Southwark around this time and reports do not tell us which gaol they were sent to. The most famous Southwark gaol was named The Clink, which became the generic name for any prison for many decades to come. However this prison was burnt down in the Gordon Riots of 1780. There were two possible destinations for our prisoners: one was the Kings Bench prison named after the court it served which was famous for the good conditions enjoyed by rich prisoners and the awful conditions endured by the poor and which later became a military prison before being closed in 1880.

The other, and therefore the most likely, was the Marshalsea. This was possibly the biggest Southwark prison for felons at this time. It was later used as the confinement for debtors before being finally abandoned in 1811. Readers might recall this was featured in the Charles Dickens television production of *Little Dorrit* starring Sir Tom Courtenay.

At their gaol in Southwark, still chained together, they would have been herded into communal cells for the two month wait for their ship to berth at Gravesend. By this time all our ladies will have known each other quite well as their fate was as common as it possibly could be.

Perhaps there might even be some kind of bond between them giving support and comfort even though their living conditions must have been somewhat hard and their prospects very uncertain. Although they would have been fairly used to life in gaol by this time, they would now be in the company of the worst of London's criminal society. This would undoubtedly add a new dimension to their daily life – an eye-opener to another life beyond their relatively quiet country experience. Then they might also have wondered about how their absent colleagues Susannah and Mary Cooper were faring.

Having spent just two months in Southwark the six convicts were transferred a day's ride down the River Thames by wagon to Gravesend on 31 January to embark on their transport the *Lady Penrhyn*. This would most likely have been their first sight of the sea so we can only wonder their thoughts and emotions at this time. At least they would be breathing fresh sea air for some while.

Conditions on board these ships are popularly believed to have been terribly cramped and horrendous. Whilst it was obviously no

Marshalsea Prison in Southwark.

picnic our ladies would have been fairly better off than others, and most certainly better that the fleets of convicts that followed. Some fortune for our eight Worcester women was that the ship to which they were assigned, the *Lady Penrhyn,* was a brand new vessel and this would be her maiden voyage. So the ship would have been clean and free of vermin and rot. It was a ship of 338 tons, built on the River Thames that year. Her master, William Cropton Sever, was part-owner with William Curtis. A London lord mayor of the 1790s affectionately known as Billy Biscuit because of his family links to sea biscuit manufacture.

The ship had already spent a month at Deptford fitting out, taking on stores and had boarded just over seventy female convicts from the nearby Newgate gaol, a gaol notorious for the reputation of its inmates. So when it sailed down river arriving at Gravesend on 29 January in order to take on twenty-two convicts from the Southwark gaol, our Worcester women, admittedly convicts in their own right, might have experienced yet another culture shock on meeting their new shipmates.

Ann, Sarah, Olivia and their colleagues would have just four days to adjust to life on board before setting sail for Portsmouth on 4 February 1787. They would arrive at the Motherbank on 10 February to wait for the rest of the fleet to assemble and prepare for the momentous voyage to New South Wales. This would take several months but just four weeks before finally weighing anchor, they would meet up once again with Mary Cooper and Susannah Hufnell who would be transferred from the *Friendship*. This would now unite all eight of the women from Worcester together for the very first time.

The *Lady Penrhyn*.

VI
IN READINESS

The pending voyage would have been a veritable nightmare to organise. To manage so many convicts would require huge manpower. Then there would be the equipment and supplies for the voyage, and also all the tools and logistics required to establish a whole settlement the other side of the globe. Livestock in the form of pigs, sheep, chickens and cows were needed for food on the voyage and more would be taken on board at each port en route. The assembling and victualling of the fleet at Portsmouth commenced early February until setting sail on 13 May.

The fleet being amassed for this historic settlement of the new 'Land beyond the Seas' would consist of eleven ships under the command of Arthur Phillip RN, namely HMS *Sirius,* the flagship of the fleet, and HMS *Supply,* one hundred and seventy-five ton, armed tender to the fleet. Then the six convict ships: *Alexander,* 452 tons, the largest convict ship; *Charlotte,* 335 tons; *Prince of Wales,* 350 tons; *Scarborough,* 450 tons; *Friendship,* 278 tons, the smallest convict ship; and *Lady Penrhyn,* 333 ton, a convict ship for women only. These were supported by the three supply ships: *Fishburn,* 378 tons, the largest store ship; *Golden Grove,* 375 tons; and *Borrowdale,* 272 tons.

Of the convict ships, two were originally slave ships requisitioned by the Royal Navy. There is very little information to be found on the layout of these ships but conditions on ships of this era are popularly believed offer very limited headroom below decks. However, research has shown that the deck to ceiling height on the *Lady Penrhyn* to be an ample five feet, ten inches which would not present a problem for the average female in those days whose height was only five feet, two inches.

Except for the *Lady Penrhyn,* the convict ships were fitted out with strong hatch bars between decks and bulkheads to divide convicts from crew. Convicts were housed below decks on the prison deck near or below the waterline and many were confined in pens to prevent trouble or even a mutiny from breaking out with some being restrained in chains only to be allowed on deck for fresh air and exercise. The female convicts would most likely have had the whole of the prisoner's deck to themselves and relative freedom above deck at certain times so long as they didn't get in the way of the crew running the ship.

Being on board a new ship was not the whole story for Ann, Olivia, Sarah and their colleagues. The fact that conditions on the *Lady Penrhyn* were much better than most other transports was also attributed to the enlightened attitude of the Commander of the fleet Arthur Phillip.

Captain Arthur Phillip RN.

A later story from a Jenny Jones, the eight-year-old daughter of Elizabeth Jones convicted of theft at the Old Bailey and accompanying her mother, relates that they climbed the ladder onto the *Lady Penrhyn* with much difficulty due to their manacles in case of escape.

They were then stripped and washed with soap and cold water and issued with new clothes. Captain Phillip was moved to report to the Admiralty that:

> The situation in which the magistrates sent the women on board the *Lady Penrhyn* stamps them with infamy. They are almost naked and so very filthy that nothing but clothing them could have prevented them from perishing. This could not be done in time to prevent a fever which is now aboard the ship where there are also many venereal complaints and several of the women are with child.

I repeat my request to increase the convict allowance of bread to 16 lb. for 42 days and supplies of fresh meat and wine for the sick.

Typhus broke out in the ships anchored there and sixteen male prisoners died on the *Alexander* as well as five female prisoners, one from the *Lady Penrhyn*. All this before they had left port. Eventually the convict ships would set sail down the English Channel on their way to Portsmouth, where it still took many months for the ships to be loaded with the rest of their supplies with the last convicts being taken on board the day the fleet sailed.

So, what would it have been like for Ann and her colleagues? During the thirteen weeks wait at the Motherbank in Portsmouth, our eight women would have been in a state of suspended anticipation. Now that Susannah Hufnell and Mary Cooper had joined their Worcester colleagues on the *Lady Penrhyn* they now had the opportunity to compare notes on their experiences since leaving Southwark Gaol. Life could continue with the ordinary everyday problems which would offer the opportunity for gossip.

It was during this period that Mary Abel would give birth to a son on 13 April whom she named William Tilley, presumably after the father, Thomas Tilley, a convict whom she would marry on 4 May 1788 in Sydney Cove. Of course, there are no diaries or convict accounts of life on board, but this could quite probably have provided a welcome distraction for our Worcester women. The newborn might have been well looked after with several 'mothers' willing to assist in his welfare, taking turns in nursing and providing warmth and care.

With no less than twelve births during the voyage, as well as several miscarriages, it seems only natural that these events as well as the progression of the pregnancies resulted in many friendships through caring and helping each other.

The *Lady Penrhyn* was a convict ship for women only so it would be inevitable that relationships with the crew would develop even though it was actively discouraged by the authorities. Fraternising with gaolers had been rife in the gaols for several reasons: to escape beatings, to get more food, to receive better treatment, possibly for the basic need for some affection and not forgetting the possibility of true romance. Conditions on the *Lady Penrhyn* would have been much more relaxed and it is during this period that Sarah Bellamy, still only seventeen years old, became involved with Joseph Downey who was the ship's Quartermaster – a responsible position which reflects on the character of the man and would have been a calming influence for the young woman.

There is a question as to whether a blind eye might have been cast to officers and those in responsible positions who fraternised with the women as it was certainly forbidden for the crew. Yet Joseph Downey managed to form a relationship and even Captain William Server was known to have formed a relationship with a convict.

The weather at this time of year would still have been fairly harsh, especially by the sea. With no heating in inclement weather and with hygiene and basic sanitation severely lacking in those times, the air below decks with so many bodies in such a confined area would not have been very pleasant even though the vessel was new. The hatches would have been secured down at night for security reasons and also during bad weather. On the other hand, it would not have been anywhere near as bad as the dark, dismal, damp cells of the gaols they had all experienced for quite a period.

Even though the ships were small, they managed to pack in quite a lot of personnel. The *Lady Penrhyn* had a crew consisting of the captain plus a crew of twenty-nine which included one cook and two surgeons – John Turnpenny Altree was surgeon to the convicts, and Arthur Bowes Smyth was surgeon to the ship's complement. Of this crew, a mate was to die before setting sail. Also on board for the eventual colonization were thirteen marines from the rank of captain down to private. Then there was a child (the son of the marine captain, a naval Lieutenant on route to China) and one James Smith, the only free passenger, a settler and first migrant. Finally the one hundred and two female convicts, some of those with a child.

The number of people directly associated with the First Fleet will probably never be exactly established, and all accounts of the event vary slightly. However, the following presents a fairly accurate guide:

Embarked at Portsmouth

Officials and passengers	15
Ships' crews	324
Marines	247
Marines wives and children	46
Convicts (men)	579
Convicts (women)	193
Convicts' children	14
Total embarked	*1,420*

Landed at Port Jackson

Officials and passengers	14
Ships' crews	306
Marines	245
Marines wives and children	54
Convicts (men)	543
Convicts (women)	189
Convicts' children	22
Total landed	*1,373*

During the voyage there were to be twenty-two births (thirteen boys, nine girls), while sixty-nine people would either die, be discharged, or desert (sixty-one males and eight females). As no complete crew musters have survived for the six transports and three store ships, there may have been as many as one hundred and ten more seamen.

There are no known detailed accounts of the voyage from the prisoner's viewpoint. However, the Assistant Surgeon commissioned to serve on the *Lady Penrhyn* – Arthur Bowes Smythe – kept a journal of his time on board including the first weeks in New South Wales. The original is now in the National Library of Australia.

In researching his manuscript on the Australian websites I happened to follow several links – one which referred me to an antiquarian bookshop in Sydney, New South Wales. I emailed the shop to see if they had anything that might help my research and was amazed that they happened to have a bound copy of A. B. Smythe's log which was currently on Ebay. This was too good to be true: I had to have it. Three days later, for a surprisingly modest sum, I had bought it. Within ten days it had arrived on my doorstep, the postage costing more than I had paid for the book!

This purchase filled in the biggest gap in my story as it gave a remarkable insight into that voyage, parts of which are reproduced in this book.

Arthur Bowes Smythe first came on board at Portsmouth on 22 March 1787. Much of his log tells of his time in Portsmouth and the ports en route, the people he met and dined with, and places he visited. Whilst interesting as background to the voyage, the majority of his entries shed scant light on the effect of the voyage on the convicts. I have extracted some of the entries that assist, which are copied verbatim, and are given below, including the abbreviations and spellings that he used.

> April 13th 1787
> This day Mr Balmain deliver'd one of the convict women on
> board the Lady Penrhyn of a boy who is likely to do very well.

The boy mentioned above was Mary Abel's son, who was conceived in Worcester gaol, and named William Tilley.

Another entry in his log in early April – when the ship was in Portsmouth Harbour awaiting fleet orders – records the order of Senior Lieutenant Johnston to keep the women from the sailors! Something must have given him cause to issue this order, but surely it would have been more appropriate to order the sailors to stay away from the women? However – ours is not to reason why! But then a later entry in his journal makes it abundantly clear why that order was issued.

> April 19th
> This night at 10 o'clock Lieuts George Johnstone & Wm
> Collins went down into the women's berths & called over the
> names of the convicts:
> Found five missing: 4 wt the sailors and one wt Squires

the 2nd Mate.

They order'd all the 5 women to be put in irons & removed forward & Mr Johnstone declar'd he wd the next day write to Major Ross at Portsmouth abt this affair & to have the 2nd Mate removed from the ship.

Weather calm.

A corpse sew'd up in a hammock floated alongside our ship.

April 26th

Rainy & squally. A corpse floated alongside. That is two corpses within 7 days – Hard to contemplate!

April 28th

Wind NW continues very high wt a great swell – the women very sick wt the motion of the ship.

May 4th

Fleet taking on bread and water in readiness for the voyage.

With the fleet now ready to sail, what of our eight women? What must have been going through their minds? Would they be thinking of their families back home, their parents, grandparents, brothers, sisters and friends, never to be seen again?

Would Ann Inett be reflecting on her two children from whom she had been separated for so long now? She would now have to face the rest of her life without them. We assume that her mother took care of Thomas and Constance who were by now aged nine and six respectively.

What about Sarah Bellamy, still only seventeen and the youngest of them all? Would she be homesick and missing the comfort of her family? She would, at least, be enjoying some kind of warmth in her new relationship with Joseph Downey.

Olivia, possibly the most daring and adventurous of them all – was she really that strong or was she now in fear of what might be before her?

On the other hand, is it possible, with all the hardship and suffering these women had suffered since their arrest and appearance in the court at Worcester, that their minds had become insensitive to such thoughts?

Undoubtedly, their lives would now follow a completely new course in which there would never again be any contact with their past. What a devastating thought!

Captain Watkin Tench, a marine detachment commander on the *Charlotte* wrote in his journal:

> Few complaints or lamentations were to be heard among them, and an ardent wish for the hour of departure seemed generally to prevail.

Now surgeon Arthur Bowes Smythe writes in his log:

> May 12th
> Fleet sails without *Lady Penrhyn, Charlotte,* and *Prince of Wales.*

> May 13th
> Remaining ships set sail.

So now the fleet raised anchor and with a fair wind finally set sail on Sunday 13 May 1787. There were 1,420 persons on eleven small ships, not just laden with stores and livestock to last until the next port, but with all the equipment, tooling and supplies needed to establish a colony of more than a thousand people.

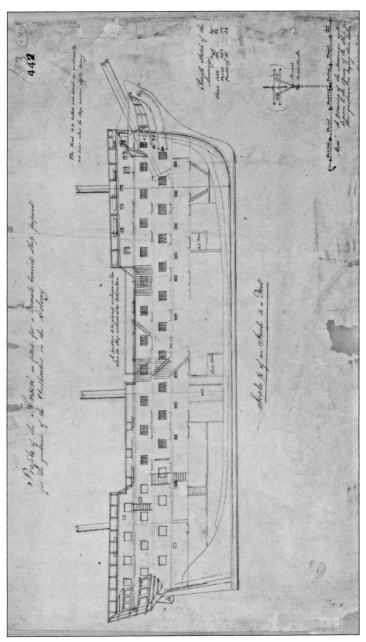

Plan of a typical convict transporter.

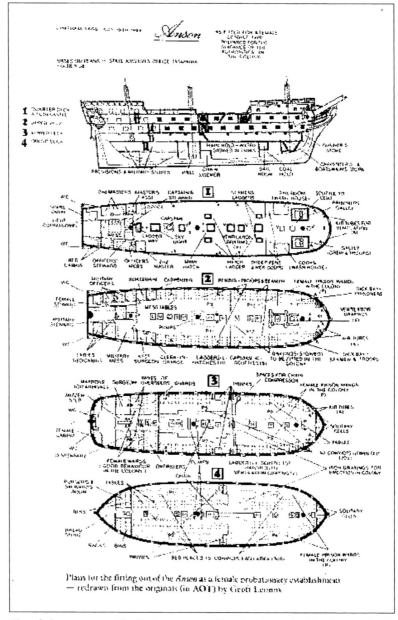

Plan of a later transport ship after it was converted to a hulk moored in Van Dieman's Land.

VII
THE VOYAGE

The itinerary for the voyage would be:

Depart	Portsmouth	Sunday 13 May 1787.
Arrive	Tenerife	Saturday 3 June 1787.
Depart	Tenerife	Saturday 10 June 1787.
Arrive	Rio de Janeiro	Monday 7 August 1787.
Depart	Rio de Janeiro	Monday 4 September 1787.
Arrive	Cape Town	Friday 13 October 1787.
Depart	Cape Town	Sunday 12 November 1787.
Arrive	Botany Bay	Friday 18 January 1788.

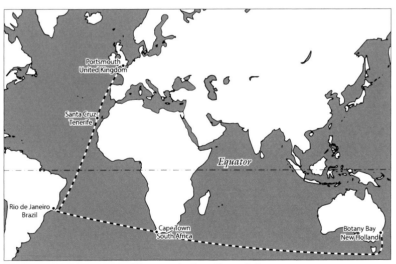

The route the First Fleet sailed.

Ship's crew and officials on the *Lady Penrhyn*.

Captain, William Cropton Sever.
Quarter masters, William Curtis/Crudis, and Joseph Downey.
Surgeon, John Turnpenny Altree.
Assistant surgeon, Arthur Bowes Smyth.
Chief mate, Nicholas Anstis/Antis.
Second mate, Mr Squires.
Third mate(s), (Thomas William Jenkinson, died before the fleet sailed), Thomas Ball.
Fourth mate, James Holmes.
Boatswain, William Gunthorpe.
Cook, Sisson (unknown).
Ship's boys, Richard Dawson, and David Duncan.
Seamen, Joshua Bentley, Charles Clay, John Clements, Edward Dean/Dease, William Curtis, John Fisher, William Henderson, Henry Hill (deserted at Rio), William Moran, Phillip Scriven, William Sodwick, Joseph Theakston, William Twiss, Thomas Shaw, William Young (steward).
Officials, James Smith (settler, the only passenger and first migrant), John Watts (naval lieutenant, passenger *en route* to China).
Family on board, James Campbell (child, relation of Captain Campbell).

Marines:
Captain, James Campbell.
Lieutenants, George Johnston, first lieutenant; William Collins, second lieutenant.
Quarter masters, William Marshall, and Charles Roach.
Privates, James Baker, Thomas Bramwell, Henry Clements, John Colthread/Coulthread, William Collins, George Gunn, George Johnston, William Simmons.

So, at last, the historic journey had begun. The female prisoners were now much better clothed than when they sailed from Portsmouth for during this initial part of the voyage Captain Phillip had ordered the sail makers on board all the vessels carrying female prisoners to improvise garments for the females. Captain Phillip was obviously well-pleased at the reigning state of affairs for in his first despatch to the Admiralty he reported that 'the convicts are not so sickly as when we sailed . . . only eight dead on route . . . the convicts behaved well.'

Having left port one day after the main fleet, it took only two days to catch up as they approached the Lizard. Surgeon Arthur Bowes Smythe's log describes a fairly leisurely life on board with sailors fishing whilst under sail, 'Many on board engaged fishing for mackerel with success'.

He also reports that day, 'A great many casks of Geneva [gin] floating' of which the *Fishburn* picked up thirty-five and the *Scarborough* picked up twenty-five. A lugger from Falmouth was also involved and he reports that all hands were very drunk.

The weather over the next four or five days deteriorated, with brisk gales, great swells and a lot of rain. This was probably the first time that our eight Worcester women had experienced bad weather at sea, but there are no records as to how they reacted. There was an attempted rising by some of the convicts on *Scarborough* which was quickly suppressed with the ringleaders being put in heavy chains, given twenty-five lashes and transferred to the *Prince of Wales*.

One curious entry in Smythe's log appears on Thursday 24 May when he writes, 'One of the Pidgeons [*sic*] went overboard and was drowned'.

It is not strange that pigeons were kept on board as they were used as a means of communication between ships. What does seem odd is how this bird managed to go overboard.

Better weather followed with crew engaged in more fishing and Surgeon Smythe reports that Marine Captain Campbell caught a large bonito (similar to tuna). Various entries in the log report the killing of a pig, the sighting of sharks, improving weather (as they are now sailing through the Bay of Biscay and approaching North Africa), and the sailor William Moran had to be treated for the lues venerea – a typical complaint for sailors no doubt. On 31 May, Mr Watts' goat had two kids, at 3 o'clock the convict Isabella gave birth to a girl, and, to round the day off, a large shark was seen near the ship.

Four days later, with the weather fine and warm, the fleet entered port at Santo Cruz for one week in which to take on supplies for the next leg of the voyage. Here fresh water, vegetables and meat were taken on board. Phillip and the chief officers were entertained by the local governor.

The master of the *Alexander* lost control of his barque when a troublesome convict John Powers headed a mutiny. This was put down by force of arms, and Powers was clamped in irons below decks for the remainder of the voyage (he was publicly hanged on landing at Port Jackson). However, his escapade only made the authorities more vigilant and any concessions granted during the twenty-four-day voyage were quickly withdrawn as a warning against any further attempts.

However, in spite of the increased vigilance, it was recognised that both crew and the prisoners needed exercise and fresh air, so during the four days the fleet was anchored at Tenerife the prisoners were allowed on deck, albeit still in chains, and the officers and marines given shore leave.

The fleet replenished its supplies whilst in port during which time each convict was allowed an extra pound of fresh meat and a pound of soft bread. Then at five o'clock in the morning of 10 June the fleet sailed for Rio de Janeiro taking advantage of favourable trade winds and ocean currents which would turn out to be a long and trying voyage.

Marine Captain Campbell seems to have been a dab hand at fishing as there are two more reports of him catching large bonito and a thirty-six-pound dolphin. There are several reports of illnesses and their treatments to the crew and officers but one in particular to the female convict Ann Read is noteworthy. On 22 June he wrote:

> This day, one of the convicts (Ann Read) took ill. I gave her a Draught of Solution of Mercury Sublimate Corrosive: instead of water – gave her a strong emetic and afterwards repeated large doses of Oleum Ricini & she did very well.

No surprise there! I am sure that had I been subjected to that treatment I would certainly declare myself cured – if only to save myself from further treatment!

On 24 June, after a period of calm, there followed a most violent storm which caused some damage around the fleet, then another period of calm with the temperature around eighty-five degrees Fahrenheit.

On 1 July, Mary Love, a sixty-year-old convict,

> fell down the steerage breaking two of her ribs and otherwise very much bruis'd herself. Cup'd her & administered the usual medicines in such cases and she perfectly recover'd. This day also Wm Henderson, sailor, rec'd a bad wound to the head from the fall of a block.

The next entries of interest in the assistant surgeon's log mention fine breezes, the sighting of many flying fish, and the traditional 'crossing of the line' ceremony whereby sailors who have never before crossed the 'Tropic of Cancer' are subjected, under the orders of 'King Neptune' to a friendly, but raucous, ducking by their more experienced colleagues.

> July 4th
> This day deliver'd Eliz Colley, one of the convicts, a dead boy.

> July 5th
> This day Mr White came on board to enquire into the state of the sick – perfectly satisfied wt the Acct & pronounced the Lady P the most healthy ship in the fleet.

> July 9th
> This day a perfectly fine Terrier dog of Mr Watts went overboard & was drown'd, supposed to have been maliciously drove over by some one in the ship: Seldom a day passes in these latitudes but Capt Campbell (whose line is constantly out) catches one or more fish.

July 11th

This day Elizth Beckford, a convict on board us, aged 82 died
of a dropsy wt wh she had long been afflicted. She died abt 9
in the Eveng & abt 10 her corpse was committed to the deep
with the usual form. The burial service was read by Mr Ball
3rd Mate.

Sat July 14th

Cross'd the Equinoxial line at exactly 12 o'clock this night –
many of the convicts fell ill of fevers this day. [One wonders if
Ann, Olivia, Sarah and the others were among the sufferers!]

Now followed a period of relatively calm seas and clement weather
during which the water allowance for convicts was increased from
three pounds to four pounds, Spruce beer was brewed for the use
of the cabin (officers only?), several whales were sighted – one of
them reported as 'enormous' – and rolls were baked every day for
breakfast.

Then came an inevitable change of weather to squalls, great swells
and heavy rain during which one unfortunate male convict on the
Alexander was lost overboard.

One week later the weather changed yet again as the fleet
approached the port of Rio de Janeiro finally dropping anchor on
Monday August 6th. The fleet stayed a month in Rio while the ships
were cleaned and water taken on board. Repairs were necessary and
Phillip ordered large quantities of food for the fleet. The women
convicts' clothing, which had become infested with lice, was burned,
and the women were issued with new clothes made from rice sacks.

While the convicts remained below deck, the officers explored
the city and were entertained by its inhabitants. A convict and local
marine were punished for passing forged quarter-dollars made from
old buckles and pewter spoons.

One event as the fleet prepared to sail involved a sailor on the
Lady Penrhyn.

A page from Arthur Bowes Smythe's Journal.

The page containing the entry concerning the lugger on which all hands were drunk.

Sept 3rd

This day Henry Hill one of our sailors, who was a Roman Catholic abt 21 years old eloped from the ship and conceal'd himself in the town. Capt Sever was not sorry at his loss as he behaved very exceptionally on board.

At daybreak on 4 September, the fleet weighed anchor and set sail for the Cape of Good Hope. The following six weeks followed much the same pattern as before but with higher temperatures being recorded. Certainly they encountered heavy seas as well as calm, damage to masts and rigging and the usual sightings of whales, albatross, flying fish and other ships from time to time.

The only noteworthy events occurred on 9 October, when a convict on the *Charlotte* was lost overboard. That same day there was a rumour of mutiny and lack of control on the *Alexander* with threats of harsh punishment when the ships docked at Cape Town.

On Saturday 13 October at precisely two minutes before 6 pm they dropped anchor in Table Bay. A beautiful bay with the Table Mountain looming high in the background. Phillip, writing to his friend Evan Nepean of the Home Office said:

> With respect to the convicts, they have all been allowed the
> liberty of the deck in the day and many during the night,
> which has kept them much healthier than could have been
> expected.

However, on their first sight of the shore, the prisoners were greeted
with the sight of, 'many gallows and implements of punishment
erected alongside the shore.'

There were wheels for breaking felons, upon several of which were
the mangled bodies of unhappy wretches who had suffered upon
them, often with their right hands cut off and fixed to the side of the
wheel. In spite of the harsh treatment that the women had both seen
and endured, this sight must have filled them with trepidation after
a relatively settled period at sea. Understandably perhaps, there were

no reported escape attempts during the month the fleet was anchored in Cape Town!

This was to be the last port of call, so the main task was to stock up on plants, seeds and livestock for their arrival in New South Wales. The livestock taken on board the ships destined for the colony of New South Wales included: two bulls, seven cows, one stallion, three mares, forty-four sheep, thirty-two pigs, four goats and 'a very large quantity of poultry of every kind'.

Women convicts on the *Friendship* had to be moved to other transports to make room for the livestock purchased there. Lieutenant Ralph Clark, a marine on the *Friendship* noted in his diary, with regard to the thirty sheep taken on board into quarters vacated by the female convicts, 'I think we will find them more agreeable shipmates than the women were!'

The convicts were provided with fresh beef and mutton, bread and vegetables to build up their strength for the rest of the journey.

The first day in port, many convicts and marines on the *Charlotte* fell ill with a kind of putrid fever and dysentery, so much so that some were not expected to last the day.

> Oct 29th
>
> The 2nd Mate (Patrick Valance) of the *Friendship,* being much intoxicated, fell overboard from the head & never came up again – he was abt 45 years of age.

> Nov 1st
>
> Phebe Norton, a convict on board us fell from the head [toilet], into the sea, it was a remarkably calm day, therefore before she had time to go down, two men jumped overboard and saved her by hauling her into the pinnacle wh she was fastened to the stern.

One wonders whether poor Phebe had time or was even able to adjust her clothing to save her modesty in front of the sailors! I bet next time she went to the toilet she would have held on very tight indeed. And what about the other hundred or so female convicts on board? I bet they had a good laugh at her expense and our ladies probably talked about it for days after.

On 11 November they sailed at one o'clock in the afternoon having victualled for the last leg and for their first weeks at their destination. The Dutch colony of Cape Town was the last outpost of European settlement which the fleet members would see for years, perhaps for the rest of their lives. Before them stretched the awesome, lonely void of the Indian and Southern Oceans, and beyond that lay nothing they could imagine.

Four days after leaving port, on 4 November, convict Ann Morton gave birth to a boy.

Convict Jane Parkinson died on 18 November.

Assisted by the gales of the latitudes below the fortieth parallel, the heavily-laden transports surged through the violent seas. Progress was again slow – storms, heavy and contrary swells and easterly winds delayed progress so much that, in November Captain Phillip was compelled to split the fleet and transfer to the brig *Supply* then, together with *Friendship, Scarborough*, and *Alexander*, hastening to prepare for the arrival of the remaining vessels that would follow at a slower rate of knots. The planned route was via the southern Indian Ocean rounding the south of Van Dieman's Land (later Tasmania), which at the time was considered to be an extension of the mainland, before sailing north into the Pacific Ocean. Consequently, the fleet sailed well to the south-east and whilst it finally encountered and took full advantage of the prevailing westerlies. The continued progress to the deep south-east took the fleet into constant rain and extreme cold which made life intolerable for the convict population confined to the lower levels of the heavily laden vessels.

One opportunity to give their situation a lift occurred on 2 December when Thomas Kelly, a convict on the *Alexander* was sent on board to superintend the governor's horses. He was found to have broached a barrel of rum and caught drinking and sharing copious amounts with a number of the female convicts below decks. It was clear that they had put him up to it and he was very lucky to have escaped punishment.

On Monday 10 December, surgeon Smythe writes at length for the very first time about the female convicts on board the *Lady Penrhyn*.

After commenting very favourably about the provisioning and treatment of the ship, officers, crew and prisoners he states:

> I wish I c'd with truth add that the behaviour of the convicts merited such extreme indulgence – but I believe I may venture to say there was never a more abandon'd set of wretches collected in one place at any period than are now to be met with in this ship in particular & I am credibly informed the comparison holds wt respect to all convicts in the fleet. The greater part of them are so totally abandon'd and callous'd to all sense of shame & even common decency that it frequently becomes indispensably necessary to inflict corporal punishment upon them, and sorry to say that even this rigid mode of proceeding has not the desired effect. Since every day furnishes proofs of their being harden'd in their wickedness – nor do I conceive it possible in their present situation to adopt any plan to induce them to behave like rational or even human beings – perpetually thieving the cloathes from each other, nay, almost from their backs may be rank'd amongst the least of their crimes (tho' it is the crime for which most of them are in their disgraceful situation) . The oaths and imprecations they daily make use of in their common conversation & little disputes with each other by far exceeds anything of the kind to be met wt amongst the most profligate wretches in London. Nor can their matchless hippocracy be equalled except by their base ingratitude; many of them plundering the sailors (who have at every port they arrived at, spent almost the whole of their wages due to them in purchasing different articles of wearing apparel & other things for their accommodation) of their necessary cloathes & cutting them up for some purpose of their own – Upon any very extraordinary occasion such as thieving fighting with each other or making use of abusive language to the Officers, they have thumb screws put on – or iron fetters on their wrists . . . and sometimes their hair has been cut off and their head shaved, which they seem to dislike more than any other punishment they underwent. At

first one or two were flog'd with a cat of 9 tails on the naked
breech; but as there are certain seasons when such a mode of
punishment c'd not be inflicted with that attention to decency
wh everyone whose province it was to punish them, wished
to adhere to, it was totally laid aside. They were also whilst
under punishment so very abusive that there was a necessity
for gag(g)ing them.

Having got that off his chest, the writer wonders whether the
'wretches' referred to had come from the notorious areas of London
where that kind of behaviour was reportedly common. As for the eight
Worcester females, it is probable that such behaviour was deprecated.
This view is supported by their eventual behaviour in the new colony.

By 20 December they had encountered sleet and the rigging was
thick with ice making navigation hazardous. Between Christmas and
New Year 1788 mountainous seas continually broke over the ships
soaking everybody and everything within them. On the night of the
thirty-first of December 1787, Bowes noted that, 'Many of the women
were washed out of their berths by the sea we had shipped. The night
was a dreadful one with the seas mounting so high that it seemed that
the ship was sometimes going over.'

However, the ship's log recorded that the high seas were, 'Not so
terrible as to reform the wicked because less than an hour after the
storms had abated, they were uttering the most horrid oaths.'

On New Year's Day, 1788, Bowes further noted that, 'The seas
became so high that it became absolutely necessary to clamp the
hatches over the convicts otherwise the ship would have been in
danger of sinking.'

In fact, one report states: 'During a dreadful period of violent
storms, most of the women were on their knees in prayer.'

What terror there would have been for Ann and her fellow female
prisoners on the *Lady Penrhyn* – clamped below decks in total darkness
and tossed from side to side as the ship plunged and rolled totally at
the mercy of the ferocious storm which raged above.

But they were not the only human cargo enduring these extreme
conditions; the crews, prisoners and livestock (taken onboard at

Cape Town) on every vessel in the fleet also experienced the same ordeal. Much of the deck cargo, including some of the livestock was also lost to the storm or had been rendered useless so Captain Phillip planned to anchor off the southern coast of Van Dieman's Land to disembark a party to cut grass to keep the remaining livestock alive, but it was too rocky and dangerous to contemplate such an operation.

In early January he rounded the southeastern coast of New Holland, but even then the currents produced the worst swells of the whole voyage and these were quickly followed by a hurricane. However, on 18 January 1788 the vanguard of the fleet entered the Bay, to be followed by the remainder of the fleet two anxious waiting days later. Finally, by 20 January 1788 all eleven ships had arrived.

Ann, Olivia and their colleagues must have been terrified at times. But they had been on one of the world's greatest sea voyages — eleven vessels carrying about 1,420 people embracing twelve nationalities (582 males, 193 females and fourteen children), with livestock and stores had travelled for 252 days for more than 15,000 miles (24,000 km) without losing a ship.

Thirty-nine male, four female convicts and three children died on the journey, but eleven of the twelve babies born during on board miraculously survived. Given the rigours of the voyage, the navigational problems, the poor conditions and sea-faring inexperience of the convicts, the primitive medical knowledge, the lack of precautions against scurvy, the crammed and foul conditions of the ships, poor planning and inadequate equipment, this was a most remarkable achievement.

One doubts whether any of this would have crossed the women's minds. But put yourself in their place. They had indeed survived a long six month arduous journey on a small creaking sailing vessel that had encountered terrible storms and heavy seas but which was now at rest in calm waters where they had at last dropped anchor in the deserted bay.

No doubt they would have been allowed on deck to survey the scene. This was going to be their home for at least the next seven years of their sentence but, more probably, the rest of their lives.

One advantage would be the climate. This would be very strange for them as they would have expected January to be cold but in this part of the world it was mid-summer and much hotter than any summer they had experienced before.

Surely they must have been so relieved that the journey was finally over and wondering what this land might hold for them, but for some it wasn't over – not quite yet!

VIII
THE NEW LAND

The fleet arrived between 18 and 20 January 1788. It had been Phillip's intention to select a suitable location, find good water, clear the ground, and perhaps even have some huts and other structures built before the others arrived. However, his 'flying squadron' reached Botany Bay only hours before the rest of the Fleet, so no preparatory work was possible. The HMS *Supply* reached Botany Bay on 18 of January 1788. The three fastest transports in the advance group arrived on 19 January with the slower ships, including the *Sirius* arriving on 20 January.

It didn't take long for the colonists to realize that Captain Cook's description of Botany Bay was, to put it mildly, a little on the fanciful side. The bay itself was open to the rough sea, there was no fresh water and the soil did not appear to be able to grow anything edible. There were trees in the area, but their wood was so tough that they had to be blasted out of the ground with gunpowder.

As a result, two days after his arrival, Captain Phillips and a scouting party left the bay in three small boats with the intention of finding a more suitable bay to the north.

On 23 January, they returned with news of a better anchorage. Phillips described it as 'the finest harbour in the world, in which a thousand sail of the line may ride in the most perfect security.' The fleet and the colonists moved to their new home on 26 January 1788 and anchored in deep water which Phillips named Sydney Cove after the British Home Secretary, Lord Sydney.

They returned to Botany Bay on the evening of 23 January, when Phillip gave orders to move the fleet to Sydney Cove the next morning.

So began several difficult days for the fleet. Unfortunately there was a huge gale blowing that day making it impossible to leave the bay, so they decided to wait until the twenty-fifth. However, during the day of the twenty-fourth they spotted the ships Astrolabe and Boussole, flying the French flag at the entrance to Botany Bay. They were having as much trouble getting into the bay as the First Fleet was having getting out. The gale was still blowing the following day when the fleet tried to leave Botany Bay, but only the HMS *Supply* managed to make it out carrying Arthur Phillip, some marines and about forty convicts; they anchored in Sydney Cove in the afternoon.

On 26 January, early in the morning, Phillip along with a few dozen marines, officers and oarsmen, finally rowed ashore and took

The First Fleet at anchor in Botany Bay.

possession of the land in the name of King George III. The remainder of the ship's company and the convicts watched from onboard the HMS *Supply*.

Meanwhile, back at Botany Bay, Captain John Hunter of the HMS *Sirius* made contact with the French ships, and he and the commander, Captain de Clonard, exchanged greetings. The *Sirius* successfully cleared Botany Bay, but the other ships were in great difficulty. The *Charlotte* was blown dangerously close to rocks; the *Friendship* and the *Prince of Wales* became entangled, both ship losing booms or sails; the *Charlotte* and the *Friendship* actually collided; and the *Lady Penrhyn* nearly ran aground. Despite these difficulties, all the remaining ships finally managed to clear Botany Bay and sail to Sydney Cove on 26 January. The last ship anchored there at about 3 pm.

The British flag was planted and formal possession was taken. This date is still celebrated as Australia Day, marking the beginnings of the first British settlement.

On arrival the male convicts were landed together with most of the

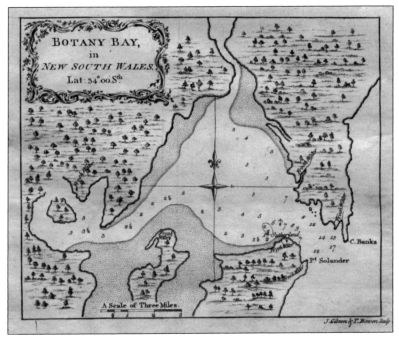

Captain Cook's map from 1773 showing Botany Bay in New South Wales.

marines. Land was cleared, a tent hospital was set up on the western side of the cove now known as The Rocks, a site for barracks was laid out nearby, and Phillip chose the site of his Government House slightly uphill south-east of the cove.

On 3 February the first religious service was held by the Revd Richard Johnson, chaplain. His text was taken from Psalm 116:12, 'What shall I render unto the Lord for all, his benefits towards me.'

One wonders what the convicts may have thought about his text that day! However, for most, those promised benefits would come their way in future years.

On Wednesday 6 February the convict women were disembarked. Arthur Bowes Smythe noted in his diary, 'We had long wished for the pleasure of seeing the last of them leave the ship. They were dressed, in general, very clean and some few amongst them might have been said to be well dressed.' He went on to record a night of debauchery, in the midst of which occurred, 'a most violent thunderstorm'.

So began the very first settlement of the new colony which was to become Australia.

First contacts were made with the local indigenous people, the Eora, who seemed curious but suspicious of the newcomers. The area was studded with enormously strong trees. Regrettably the primitive huts built for the officers and officials quickly collapsed in rainstorms. The marines had a habit of getting drunk and not guarding the convicts properly and their Commander Major Robert Ross drove Phillip to despair with his arrogant and lazy attitude. Little wonder that Phillip worried that his fledgling colony was exposed to attack from the Aborigines or foreign powers. However, he need not have worried because three years later, in 1791, Governor Phillip would write to Lord Sydney:

> 'I can still say with great truth and satisfaction that the convicts, in general, behave better than ever could have been expected and that their crimes, with very few exceptions, have been confined to the procuring for themselves, the common necessaries of life

In 1797, John Hunter, the second governor of the colony, reported to Lord Sydney:

> The vast number of women for whom we have had little work are a heavy weight on the stores of Government – if we estimate their merits by the charming children with which they have filled the colony, then, they deserve our care.

The present situation though, was still not ideal. Sydney Cove, despite its great location still offered problems to the new settlers. It did not have the raw materials needed to re-equip and maintain the ships. There was a need for supplies not available in the new territory. Large pines for masts, flax for canvas etc. Fortunately, it so happened that Captain Cook had seen these very items in abundance on Norfolk Island during his second voyage.

The First Fleet in Sydney Cove.

Governor Phillip deemed it essential that another colony should be set up on Norfolk Island in order to provide for these requirements. It is at this point that two of our subjects follow a different course, for the time being at least.

IX
NORFOLK ISLAND

So, towards the end of February 1788 the brig *Supply,* the smallest ship in the fleet, was despatched under command of Second Lieutenant Gidley King in order support the main colony.

King had the daunting task of setting up a new colony on a tiny remote, but very fertile volcanic island in the middle of an enormous expanse of the South Pacific Ocean.

Being 1,042 miles from Botany Bay the voyage would take another two weeks arriving on 6 March 1788

The occupation of the island was to serve two ends. To make available masts and sails from pine and flax for the refurbishment of British ships, and also to prevent the island falling into the hands of His Majesty's rivals – the French.

His crew consisted of: James Cunningham, master's mate from HMS *Sirius;* John Turnpenny Altree, surgeon from the *Lady Penrhyn;* Thomas Jamison, surgeon and first mate from HMS *Sirius;* Roger Morley, sailor from HMS *Sirius;* William Westbrook, sailor from HMS *Sirius;* Charles Heritage, marine; John Batchelor, marine.

Phillip's instruction to Lieutenant Gidley King with regard to the convicts was to, 'make choice of both sexes whose characters stand fairest and whose skills would be of most use.'

A contemporary report said of the motley 759 persons who arrived with the First Fleet, these fifteen were selected as, 'The best of a bad lot'. Nine males were chosen: Nathaniel Lucas and Edward Garth both from the *Scarborough;* Charles McLennan from the *Alexander,* just fourteen years old; Richard Widdicombe, aged seventy-two years (a surprise choice was the oldest of the group); John Mortimore, Noah

The brig *Supply.*

Mortimer, Edward Westlake, John Rice, and John Williams, all from the *Charlotte.*

Six females were chosen, all for their good behaviour on the voyage: Ann Inett, Elizabeth Colley, Elizabeth Lee, Olivia Gascoigne, Elizabeth Hispley, all from the *Lady Penrhyn;* Susannah Gough, from the *Friendship.*

So, once again, Ann and Olivia find their futures and fortunes entwined. Surely they must be firm friends by now.

Life was not going to be easy on the island. To start with it was a very difficult place to land – with rocks, high cliffs and then dense forests. Having spent four days circumnavigating the island looking for a suitable landing place one was found on the southern side between the reefs at what became known as Sydney Bay. They landed there without any difficulty on a fine sandy beach, although they were still faced with dense forestry.

The men did the heavy work of felling trees, clearing the ground and splitting and sawing the pines for building timber; the women did the lighter work of dragging away boughs and brushwood, preparing the ground for planting and the general cooking duties.

Before leaving Port Jackson, Phillip had appointed Gidley King Superintendent and Commandant of Norfolk Island. On landing King set about providing security for himself, the people and the provisions with a firm set of rules by which all would have to abide. His next priority was to set about establishing an ordered colony by the building of accommodations, the planting of crops and to organise the supply of flax and pine for the main colony back at Port Jackson.

The first crops perished from the wind, the salts and rats which ate the vegetables. Then they had to cope with cutworms, black caterpillars and the bright, screaming seed-eating indigenous birds. Despite the deep rich soil, after two years' hard work they had but about fifty acres of land under the hoe. Hardly what had been implicitly promised by Captain Cook and expected by Captain Phillip.

Gidley King would need someone to look after his welfare with regard to keeping his house, cooking and cleaning and so on. To this end he chose Ann Inett. Clearly she could not have been without appeal as she was described as, 'an attractive woman, small framed, dark haired, and with a neat and clean appearance.' She accepted Gidley King's offer to be his housekeeper and, according to records, proved to be, 'an industrious and accommodating woman, keeping all the public quarters clean and tidy as well as cooking Gidley King's food, keeping his home comfortable, and warming his bed at night.'

This 'onerous duty' clearly developed as she would become Gidley King's mistress and, eventually presented Commandant King with the settlement's first child.

From Ann's point of view, she was one of just twenty-two people whose task it was to help form a settlement, build dwellings, live off the land with limited supplies and to build a life from absolutely nothing. After such a traumatic period in her life, it was at this point that Ann's fortunes had changed for the better. Not that life was easy – far from it – but everything is relative and must be judged against what had gone before. Her new life had to be infinitely better to the prospects that she had left in England. As a bonus, the weather, although the region's autumn, must have been a great improvement.

Fortunes were also changing for her colleague Olivia Gascoigne. Liaisons between male and female convicts were encouraged in order to build a thriving colony – especially if they were of good behaviour. Hence, within a few weeks of their arrival, Olivia must have been attracted in some way to Nathaniel Lucas as they were married in a civil ceremony shortly after arriving on the island (more about him later).

After the initial clearing of the land for the settlement, essential buildings were erected 'log cabin' style with thatched roofs. Attention

The remains of Ann's cottage on Norfolk Island.

was then turned to the valley to the north where the soil was very fertile and through which ran a fine creek. With the sub-tropical climate their crops of wheat, corn and vegetables would thrive.

The settlement on the island would naturally grow in order to provide for the needs of the main colony in New South Wales. More convicts, more marines to control them, and the natural expansion of the settlement to other parts of the island. As a result, Ann and Olivia would eventually be joined by their old colleagues Sarah Davies, Mary Cooper, Susannah Hufnell and Mary Turner.

The first was Sarah Davies who arrived on the island in February 1789 just eleven months after the first landing. She was followed nine months later by Mary Cooper. Then in March 1790, Susannah Hufnell and Mary Turner arrived.

Was there a grand re-union? Did they renew acquaintances? Nothing is recorded so we can but wonder – however, considering the number of convicts that were being sent out to New South Wales, it does seem quite a coincidence that six of the eight women who went through the cells and courtroom of the Worcester Guildhall should all eventually be part of the colony on this tiny island in the Pacific on the other side of the world.

X
THE NEW LIFE AND BEYOND

So what became of our eight Worcester female convicts? Did they continue acquaintanceships or even become friends? No-one knows for sure, but to live in such a small community it would be odd if they didn't see each other again as the colonies were quite small in those early years. We do, at least, know where they all went.

Not a great deal is known about Abel, Cooper, Davies, Hufnell and Turner but, apart from what has already been written, we do know the following.

Mary Abel's history seems quite logical and reasonably recorded even though it may be sparse. However, there is one big question that I have been unable to resolve. What follows is all clearly documented except for one big question – Why would Mary use the name Tilley as an alias at her trial?

It would be unusual for her to have known a Thomas Tilley from Stafford, several days journey away from her own community where she grew up. Then for them both to commit crimes in those separate communities, for them both to be sentenced to transportation, for them both to end up on the same voyage to the other side of the world and then to marry would be a massive coincidence.

Whatever the answer to that question is, she did marry Thomas Tilley at Sydney Cove on 4 May 1788. He was a forty-two-year-old from Staffordshire, convicted of stealing a flaxen bag and six pieces of cloth. The son named William that she bore on the *Lady Penrhyn* whilst at anchor in Portsmouth was obviously conceived while in gaol in Worcester, possibly from a liaison with another prisoner but more likely with a gaoler. Unfortunately the child died just two weeks after her marriage to Thomas.

Mary died six years later and was buried at Sydney Cove on 21 July 1788.

Mary Cooper spent nearly two years in the colony where she bore a daughter, Elizabeth, on 12 April 1790, just a few months before being sent to Norfolk Island on 11 November of the same year. Here she would probably have renewed her relationship with Ann, Olivia and Sarah Davies. Sadly, the child died on 8 May 1792. We know that in June 1794 she was in the employ of Robert Ruth, but seems to have returned to Port Jackson at some time prior to 1802. Records show that in 1804 she was living with a soldier, Joseph Craddock, and one son.

Mary Craddock, age given as sixty-four, was buried at St Phillips, Sydney in July 1814.

Sarah Davies was married on 7 June 1788 to Thomas Restell Crowder. He was a seaman sentenced in Bristol to transportation for life under his real name – Risdale. The only records showing for her tell that on 14 November of that year, she and Crowder were charged with 'making a disturbance in the night'. Thomas was reprimanded and Sarah ordered to work for one month.

They were both sent to Norfolk Island in February 1789. Did Sarah meet up with Ann and Olivia? Very likely indeed as this settlement was a very small one.

Thomas must have acquitted himself well as Lieutenant Governor King recommended him for the position of overseer due to his good behaviour. On 3 November 1792 he was emancipated and, much to his credit, sworn in as a constable, becoming a settler and acquiring fourteen acres of land.

Unfortunately, in January 1794 he became involved in a fracas at the playhouse with a sergeant, and was arrested and kept in irons until taken to Sydney the following March. In due course he returned to the island but Sarah had died alone on 26 June 1794 aged thirty-seven. It would be nice to think that her past friends attended her funeral.

Ann had long left the island but Olivia, Mary Cooper and Susannah Hufnell were still on the island at the time.

The first record of Susannah Hufnell is at the baptism of her daughter by Corporal William Baker on 1 January 1789. Corporal Baker had been a marine on the *Charlotte*, but clearly this liaison had not blossomed as she and her daughter were sent to Norfolk Island in the March of 1790. One can only speculate as to whether she knew of Ann's return to Port Jackson just prior to her departure, but she was now, once again, in the same community as Olivia, Sarah Davies and Mary Cooper.

The next record of her shows that in February 1791, she shared a sow with a James Clark. This sow produced a litter of three in the May making them independent for meat. So did this mean that she shared more than the sow with James? Quite possibly, because she bore two more daughters – Frances born in 1793 and Sarah born on 18 July 1795.

We know that she was still on the island in 1805 but it was in this year that the colony on the island was officially abandoned by the governor back in Port Phillip. It had now served its purpose as the main colony was now self sufficient. She is believed to have formed a relationship with Aaron Davis, a convict who came out on the *Charlotte*. Her last known appearance is dated 1811 in New South Wales.

We know that Mary Turner/Wilkes shared a hut with a Mary Phillips in Pert Jackson in 1788. On 5 March 1789 she was charged together with Tamsin Allen for stealing six cabbages from the garden of William Parr. Both were ordered fifty lashes, twenty-five then followed by twenty-five on the next provision day.

On 25 March 1789 she gave evidence at the trial of the seven marines who were hanged on 27 March for stealing from the stores. Captain James Campbell suspected her of perjury and was outraged to find on 25 April that she was not in custody which led to an icy exchange of letters and complaints involving Campbell, David Collins, Major Ross and the governor.

On 4 March 1790 she was sent to Norfolk Island to join Olivia, Mary Cooper, Sarah Davies and Susannah Hufnell, where she remained unrecorded until 1793 when she returned to Port Jackson. Mary certainly seems to have had some affinity with the judicial process because she is recorded yet again as being a witness at another trial on 4 April 1797. Then in 1780 she was living with a David Batty with two sons and one daughter all said to be illegitimate. Mary died aged forty-four in Sydney, her burial registered at St Phillips on 21 January 1808.

Sarah Bellamy had a liaison with the sailor Joseph Downey shortly after arriving on the *Lady Penrhyn* at Gravesend and whilst waiting for the eventual departure from Plymouth. She gave birth towards the end of the voyage, the boy named and baptised Joseph after the father, died on 1 February 1788, just one month after arriving at the new territory. Regretfully the relationship with Downey did not survive.

Unlike her colleagues, Sarah never left the colony. Once landed, Captain Arthur Phillip started to organise the establishment of the new colony. One of his first actions was to divide the women into two categories – those who were considered able and willing to contribute positively, and those considered quite useless.

Sarah obviously fell into the first category as she was housed in a small two-room hut on the east side of Sydney cove, an area reserved mainly for naval officers, where she worked as a domestic help for a Lieutenant Faddy. Her dwelling is recorded as having two doors, a window and a hearth for a fire. She did have one more brush with the law when she was called to appear in court again under Governor Phillips' jurisdiction for disturbing the peace.

There is an almost farcical story describing this incident more fully in a booklet released by the Belbroughton History Society . . . but briefly:

One evening following a dinner party at the governor's residence, two acquaintances of Sarah – Marine Officer Captain James Meredith and Mr James Keltie (master of the *Sirius*) decided to call on her. Captain Meredith had tried to force his way into her hut through the window beneath which lay her bed, his legs supported by James Keltie. It is likely that they had eaten and drunk well by this time and anticipated a warm welcome. For whatever reason, Sarah refused them entry. The men pleaded with her and Mr Keltie had said that he merely wanted to sleep on the hearth stone – not to sleep with her. His colleague Captain Meredith was more belligerent and tried to force entry through a window. The situation then escalated with a small girl also staying in the hut with Sarah hearing Sarah's cries pleading with them to go away, and joining in the screaming. Eventually, Keltie tried to persuade Meredith to leave but without success. Meredith was intent on entering Sarah's bed. He reached through the window as far as he could pulled her head covering off and, pulling her by the hair, tried to beat her. Sarah retreated and Meredith lost his hat at which he shouted, 'You terrible faggot of a thing, give me my hat!'

Having given him his hat, Sarah hoped Meredith would go away as he had a woman of his own (Mary Johnson) at home. Meredith was not to be discouraged and, furiously continued swearing, 'I will have my revenge on you, I would no more mind killing you than I would flying in the air.'

There were cries and shouts of 'murder' heard by neighbours including an officer of the watch. Meredith ordered her to be taken to the guardhouse. Sarah then opened the door saying to Meredith that, 'He was a Gentleman, and she but a poor prisoner, therefore she must go where he bade her, but she did not know what she had done, that he had come and disturbed her peace.'

Leaving the scene, Meredith commented to John Harris, the officer of the watch, 'That he supposed there would be the Devil and all to pay the next day about this Cry of Murder.'

To cut a long story short, the criminal court was convened. This would not be a comfortable time for Sarah. Bearing in mind she was a deported convict supposed to 'possess neither virtue nor honesty' having to defend herself against the word of two senior naval personnel, and before a jury, part of which might well be colleagues of the accused, would have seemed impossible. However, with the odds stacked against her, she won her case. Meredith was sent to Norfolk Island and Keltie returned to sea.

In spite of this last brush with the law, her life began to turn for the better. It must have been around this time that Sarah met the convict James Bloodworth and their liaison would offer her stability and support. He was a convicted felon from Kingston-upon-Thames, the son of Robert Bloodworth and Ann Baker. He was married to June Marks in Shoreditch on 9 December 1782 and had three children with a fourth on the way when he was incarcerated. He had been convicted at Kingston-upon-Thames in 1785 for stealing one fighting cock and two hens and sentenced to seven years' transportation arriving at Botany Bay on the *Charlotte*.

James was a builder, a skill in high demand in this fledgling community. He was obviously industrious and must have shown responsibility and character because he progressed to supervising and training others, and was instrumental in the building programme.

Sarah's modest dwelling had probably been built by James with whom she later bore a son baptised James Bellamy Bloodworth on 17 October 1790. Sarah and James would go on to have eight children, losing four of them in infancy. They would become a highly respected couple in the community. Marriage was out of the question at this time as James had left a wife in England at the time of his transportation. It is not known if they ever officially married later.

His ambition and determination paid off as he was soon appointed master bricklayer to the settlement and would be instrumental in the building of soldiers barracks and municipal buildings as well as houses for the Surveyor General and Judge Advocate. He also built several private homes besides designing them. His buildings were solid but of crude Georgian architecture. Bloodworth can be credited with the first Government House, which lasted from 1788 to 1845 and in 1790 the storehouse at King's Wharf on the shore of Sydney Cove. Governor Phillip praised, 'the pains he had taken to teach others the business of a bricklayer', and his conduct was exemplary at a time when most convicts were noted for indolence or rebelliousness.

In 1790 he was pardoned and free to return to England, but bound himself to an agreement with Governor Phillip to work for two years, stipulating that he be clothed and fed in that time. By 1794 he was overseeing works at Sydney, Parramatta, and Toongabbie. His skill and industry earned him a grant of fifty acres at Petersham Hill and he later increased his holdings to two hundred and twenty-five acres. By 1802 he had thirty-five acres cleared with ten acres in wheat and maize. Sarah, too, had served her term and she received a grant of twenty acres in her own right.

By 1802 he had become a sergeant in the Sydney Loyal Association, a local militia of free settlers and emancipated convicts. A great sign of respect for a former convict.

During her time in New South Wales there is a good chance that Sarah and Mary Abel would have kept up with the comings and goings of their colleagues to Norfolk Island. Most certainly she would have been well aware of Ann's exploits and would eventually renew her relationship with Olivia when her life would take a turn for the worse.

Sarah's husband died of pneumonia in March 1804. At the time of his death, James was owed a great deal of money and he had invested heavily in the purchase and development of their farm. All this left him insolvent with Sarah, his de facto wife, three daughters and a son in financial difficulties. The nearest thing to a state funeral was provided, the Sydney Loyal Association escorting the body to the town cemetery where he was buried with full military honours.

Coincidentally, it would be Olivia's husband Nathaniel, living on Norfolk Island and in much the same position as James, who would be offered James' position as building superintendent and overseer. A position that he would decline.

The year following his demise Sarah rented one of her rooms with the kitchen for eighteen months to a Jeremiah Cavanaugh in return for his undertaking to teach her four children to read. Records for the following years describe Sarah as a widow, single, self employed and householder. In 1828 she was a 'washerwoman' in Phillip Street, Sydney working for a Sarah Burgess.

Sarah died at Lane Cove New South Wales on 4 February 1843 attaining the grand age for those days of seventy-three She, too, was buried at St Phillips cemetery at St Phillips. She had outlived all her colleagues.

Due to the wealth of speculation concerning Olivia Gascoigne's rumoured aristocratic background, I have devoted my last, brief chapter to these possibilities. Whatever the reality might be, Olivia's story, together with that of her eventual husband, is remarkable as it illustrates and sows the seeds of doubt in the popular concept that all those sentenced in the English courts were criminals and the dregs of society.

Within a few weeks of her arrival on the island, Olivia had met Nathaniel Lucas, become better acquainted, formed a relationship and married in a civil ceremony. This, in itself is interesting as she was the only convict allowed to marry on Norfolk Island prior to 1794 (she married in 1788). Why? Some still argue that this was possibly because she was of the privileged class, but that theory is still highly speculative.

Strange also that many generations later Queen Victoria's son, the Duke of Edinburgh, privately spent half a day with the family of Olivia's son, John, at a hotel in Burwood (Sydney) during his visit to Australia in 1866.

Officially, reported events like these reinforce Olivia's aristocratic credentials. However, it is quite possible that, due to the lack of proper recording, poor communication, and that many of these stories were passed by word of mouth, they have eventually been accepted as 'fact'. In the meantime we will have to await further research that may shed more light on the controversy.

Anyway, back to their arrival on Norfolk Island. Olivia's husband, Nathaniel Lucas, was born in 1764 in Surrey the son of a builder. Although not wealthy the family would have been comfortably off as were many trades' folk of the time. Nathaniel was a skilled carpenter, boat builder and millwright. He had clearly had some education as he was able to write and sign his own name.

At the age of twenty, employed by a builder in London, he was living in rooms above a public house in Holborn. He kept to himself and apparently failed to patronise the public bar which no doubt must have irritated the publican's wife. Did she seek revenge for his lack of patronage? Whatever the reason, there was a confrontation

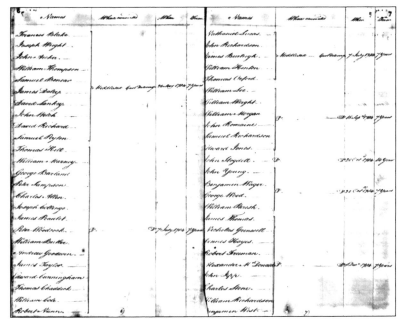

Nathaniel's entry (top of the right-hand column) in the transportation log.

between the two of them causing her to demand payment of his rent earlier than had been agreed. Nathaniel refused, and the next morning found himself awakened by a court constable, the publican and a neighbour, who on searching his 'unlockable' room found an apron, a towel, a shawl and six muslin caps belonging to the neighbour's daughter stuffed under the mattress. He was accused of the theft of items to the value of two pounds and sentenced to seven years transportation.

Is it really likely that he would have stolen such items? Hardly, but they served the purpose of the publican's wife which is indicative of many injustices of the time. As a result of no police force and no investigation of crime whatsoever, the courts had to rely on the two sides of the argument and decide which one to believe. That onus of belief invariably fell in favour of the accuser, the richest or the most eloquent. Rough justice indeed!

As a result Nathaniel ended up the other side of the world on Lt

Gidley King's expedition to colonise Norfolk Island. During their time on the island, he and Olivia seemed to have lived their life with a quiet and industrious dignity. Neither he nor Olivia had any punishments recorded against them in official journals. In their favour, Nathaniel's experience and skills as a carpenter would have been very much prized in the setting up of the colony and we know that his work was highly appreciated by the Commandant Gidley King.

This will account for his being granted fifteen acres of land at Grenville Valley where, together with Olivia and their increasingly large family, they farmed and produced wheat, maize and pork. The Lucas family increased their holdings by buying further land from settlers who later returned to Sydney.

We assume that life was more than tolerable as Olivia had eleven children while living on Norfolk Island.

In many ways, Nathaniel's life took very much a similar path to that of James Bloodworth, the partner of Olivia's colleague Sarah Bellamy, back in Sydney. While on Norfolk Island Nathaniel was responsible for building many of the settler's

Plaque at the resting place of Mary and Sarah Lucas in Emily Bay.

homes, administrative buildings and other infrastructure. After his sentence expired he acquired two further land grants and, remarkably for a convict, he too was made a constable. His fortunes continued to prosper for he was granted a water supply contract for the colony and continued to acquire more land by taking over grants which had been abandoned by less successful farmers.

However, tragedy struck the couple 15 August 1792. In order to facilitate clearing some land, he lit several huge old pines in the vicinity of his newly built house. He was horrified when a freak wind gust caused one tree to fall directly onto the house completely demolishing it. Olivia, her two-year old twins Mary and Sarah, and baby William were inside. The twins were killed instantly and Olivia sustained life-threatening injuries. William, who was being nursed by his mother miraculously escaped injury. Mary and Sarah were laid to rest at Emily Bay.

Olivia slowly recovered but it is said that she subsequently always walked with a limp. The incident was significant enough for Lieutenant Governor King to record it in his daily journal. Nathaniel was clearly devastated by this terrible loss and it is very apparent that he was still greatly affected by it when four years In 1796 he wrote his first letter home. The following letter was written to his father but never delivered:

> Sydney
> Norfolk Island
> New South Wales
> 30th October 1796

Dear Father,

    After so long an absence, an account of my state of health and situation will no doubt be pleasing to you, and I have the pleasing satisfaction to acquaint you that me and my family are all in good health and thank God and my own industry very comfortably situated. My family at present time consists of my wife and four children, two boys and two girls. I had the unspeakable misfortune to lose twin girls by an accident which could it be represented in a proper manner would awaken the most tender feelings and melt the hardest heart into sympathy. It was by the fall of a pine tree which stood near my house which buried my lovely infants in the ruins and almost my worthy partner who nearly escaped with her life for she was dragged out in a situation in which her life was despaired of. O' father I am not able to express the poignant grief felt on this very shocking scene – without dwelling long upon this displeasing subject together with a variety of misfortunes, liable to those who transgress the laws of their country – I can now with truth assert that I have surmounted them all, and with the blessing of God, I hope to in the course

of two years to return to my native country with a competency
for life.

Olivia and Nathaniel never did return to England. They remained
on Norfolk Island for another eight years until 1804 when King,
who by that time was governor of New South Wales, had invited
Nathaniel to Sydney Cove to erect a windmill for the Government.
The governor probably did this aware that within a year he would
abandon the colony on Norfolk Island. It had served its purpose as the
settlement at Sydney was now well provided for. This move coincided
with the death of the Colony's Superintendent of Carpenters – James
Bloodworth. Nathaniel accepted the contract and then went into
business for himself.

So now Olivia finally leaves Susannah Hufnell the last of the
Worcester women on the island and joins the community in which Sarah
Bellamy, as the partner of the colony's main Building Superintendent,
will have enjoyed. Olivia and the children joined Nathaniel and set up
home at Church Hill (now in Sydney city centre) where they operated
the government mill. The land on which St Philips Anglican Church
now stands was once owned by Nathaniel Lucas. Also built by him
were the Rum Hospital (now the Mint Building) and the parsonages
at Parramatta and Liverpool.

By 1810 Nathaniel had been established as a successful tradesman
and a sound businessman. Unfortunately their marriage eventually
broke up in 1816 and Olivia, with six of her children, made the decision
to move to Port Dalrymple in Van Diemen's Land.

Between 1815 and 1818 Nathaniel had many Government building
contracts, the last of which was for the construction of St Luke's
Church at Liverpool. The architect for the project was a Francis
Greenway. Nathaniel and Greenway clashed violently and frequently.
It is said that while Governor Macquarie was laying the foundation
stone of St Luke's, Nathaniel and Greenway were quarrelling so loudly
that the governor's speech was all but drowned out. A few weeks
after this, Nathaniel had left for Parramatta but never arrived at his
destination. His body was eventually discovered in mud beside the
Georges River by his son, who had been searching for him,

Olivia was convinced that Greenway had murdered him, but the circumstances of Nathaniel's death will probably never be truly known. There is no record of an inquest having been held.

For Olivia a saga had now ended. After settling Nathaniel's affairs Olivia lived in Launceston where in 1824 she was granted a hundred acres of land at Port Dalrymple in her own right. But it was around this time that the Lucas empire began to unravel. William and Nathaniel Junior's fine self-built barque, the Olivia, was wrecked near Twofold Bay with its cargo of grain and William and John's building business in Sydney collapsed. William died in suspicious circumstances in Sydney Harbour – his body was never found. Olivia lost everything as all her effects went under the hammer to pay the family debts as she had stood as guarantor for her sons.

Her eventful and productive life, having given birth to thirteen children, came to an end in Van Diemens Land when, on 10 June 1830 at the age of sixty-nine, she passed away. She was buried in the Cypress Street Cemetery in Launceston. It is to her memory that her descendants make up the largest family group in Australia today.

Ann Inett had no doubt been pleased to accept the position of housekeeper to the most important and influential person in the colony, Lieutenant Gidley King. It would have offered her protection and security the like of which she had never known in her life. She was obviously looked upon well by her benefactor and a life of domesticity followed. To the extent that while the new settlement was still in its infancy, Ann bore a child with Gidley King and the entry in the records stated, 'The eighth ushered a male child into the world and as he was the first born on the island, he was given the name "Norfolk".' And so he was baptised at divine service on 18 January 1789. The first birth of note for this fledgling colony.

At the end of that year, Gidley King was appointed commandant of the island but not long after, on 25 February 1790, he was recalled to the mainland by Governor Phillip. So Gidley King sailed from Norfolk Island taking Ann with him, now pregnant with their second child, arriving at Port Jackson in Sydney Cove on 5 April.

It had soon become apparent to Governor Phillip that further settlements both inland and along the coast were essential if the Colony was to have a long term future. As a result, on 17 April less than two weeks after returning to the mainland, Phillip despatched Gidley King as his personal emissary to England to plead the case for greater and urgent material support for the fledgling colony. This must have been a disappointment for Ann as she was now left to complete the remaining years of her sentence in the harsher penal climate of Port Jackson.

Governor Phillip had pressed ahead with his expansion plans for the colony and Rose Hill was settled in November 1788. Thus the foundations of the major settlement of Parramatta were laid. By mid-1790, there was both a substantial military and female convict presence at Rose Hill and this would have been the obvious destination for Ann to complete the remaining years of her sentence. However, this was not to be – at least, not initially. Ann was seven months pregnant on her return to the mainland and it is inconceivable that Gidley King would have allowed her and his two children to be treated like any other convict and consigned to the crowded convict huts which had been built at Rose Hill.

Ann must have remained in Sydney under the protection of the absent Gidley King as Ann's second child, again a son, was born on 25 June 1790. The child was baptised Sydney King Inett at St Phillip's Church in Sydney town on 9 July 1790. It was recorded that Sydney was the, 'son of Philip Gidley King, late Commandant of Norfolk Island and Ann Inett, Convict'.

King arrived in England on 29 December 1790 and whilst there was promoted to the rank of commander and also to lieutenant governor of Norfolk Island. Whilst back in England, Gidley King entered a marriage contract with his cousin Anna Josepha Coombe. This took place just one week before returning to Port Jackson to report to Governor Phillip on the outcome of his visit. With so little time in England this must have been either a whirlwind courtship or more possibly an arranged marriage. Clearly it was a sympathetic union as his wife was already eight months pregnant when they arrived in Australia in September 1791.

The couple spent five weeks in Sydney Town before departing for Norfolk Island to take up his enhanced command. During this time both he and his wife would have had to face up to the reality of how to plan the future of the two Inett-King boys – Norfolk who he had known and supported during the first sixteen months of his life and who was now some two years and nine months old, and Sydney whom he had never seen and who was now sixteen months old.

There had never been any doubt of the paternity of the children. This had been clearly shown by Gidley King's open relationship with Ann Inett on Norfolk Island and Sydney's baptismal entry in the register of St Phillip's Church in July 1790. This would have been common knowledge in the Colony and, no doubt, many were interested to see just how he would reconcile his pre-marital paternal responsibilities with his new executive status and with his new wife who was now pregnant with their own first child.

Lieutenant Governor Gidley King.

To his everlasting credit, and fully supported by his wife who was said to be very understanding in regard to Ann Inett and King's two illegitimate children offering to take both into her care, Gidley King's solution was to accept full responsibility for the two boys and to plan for an education for them both in England. Thus it was decided, presumably in conjunction with Ann, that both boys would be raised by the Gidley Kings and when they sailed for Norfolk Island in the 'Atlantic' on 26 October 1791 they were accompanied by little Norfolk Inett with a tacit understanding that Sydney King Inett was to join them on the island at a later date.

For the second time in her life Ann was to lose her children. Her son and daughter the other side of the world, then her two sons into a new world which she could never share or be part of. Still as boys, Norfolk and Sydney King were eventually sent to England by their father to be educated, and both went on to become distinguished Royal Navy officers.

There are no records telling of Ann's life on the mainland until 16 November 1792 when Ann entered the next significant chapter of her life by marrying one Richard John Robinson. John was a 'Second Fleeter', who had been sentenced to death at the February 1787 Old Bailey Sessions for the theft of a bay gelding. His guilt was questionable and he had been held in Newgate gaol for two and a half years under temporary respite from execution. He was eventually embarked on the *Scarborough* on 10 November 1789, one of six ships sailing on 17 January 1790 and arriving in Sydney Cove on 20 June of that year – a voyage on which twenty-six per cent of the convict population died in passage and nearly forty per cent of whom were dead within eight months of arrival in the Colony.

They were married at St Johns Church at Parramatta on 18 November 1792 by the Revd Richard Johnson. The Revd Johnson and his wife had travelled in the *Golden Grove* with the First Fleet and played an important role in the spiritual and social life of the community. He would certainly have baptised Sydney King Inett at St Phillip's Church in Sydney Town in July 1790. It is quite possible that Gidley King had arranged for Ann and their children to be placed in the Johnson household as a domestic help, or even companion to Mrs Johnson, pending his return from England.

Ann's husband-to-be had almost daily contact with the Rev Johnson and had, in effect, become his right-hand man and general factotum. He had also been registered as witness at many of the Reverend's marriage services. This is probably how he and Ann had met and become acquainted.

This period of Ann's life must have felt bitter-sweet as she had lost her children but found a new partner to offer support and comfort. It could have been even more stressful for her as it was in the period during which she handed over her children that her mother passed away back in England. She would have been unaware of this so her marriage would not have been dampened by the news.

Following marriage, their life together was both comfortable and respectable. On 23 August 1794 with her seven year sentence completed, Ann received a thirty-acre land grant in her own name from Lieutenant Governor Francis Grose known as Pleasant Farm, one of the Northern Boundary Farms established just to the north of Parramatta and Toongabbie. Their financial situation was obviously blossoming as they also opened a hotel called the Yorkshire Grey and did well over the ensuing five years.

Parramatta had grown considerably and by 1798 boasted no less than five hotels. Their household then included two servants; they owned twenty-five pigs and had twenty-two acres ready for planting maize. However, by the next year they were ready to move on and in July 1801, the couple assigned the titles of their properties to secure debts on Pleasant Farm (£160 including a £40 mortgage), Wherit's Farm (£50 debt including a £40 mortgage) and their premises in Parramatta (£70 debt).

Philip Gidley King had by then returned to Sydney in 1800 having replaced John Hunter as governor of the colony and the Robinson's fortunes continued to improve under his stewardship. They relocated to Sydney Town after leaving Parramatta and on 2 April 1804 Governor King awarded them a fourteen-year land grant which was annotated, 'Instead of Rich'd John Robinson this lease is given in the name of Ann Robinson – by His Excellency's Command.' Very shortly afterwards on 18 June 1804, Governor King granted Richard John Robinson a free pardon and on 25 November of that year the Sydney Gazette carried a notice stating:

EATING HOUSE, PITT'S ROW

Richard John Robinson begs to inform his Friends and the Public in general that he intends opening an Eating House at the Yorkshire Grey to commence on Thursday next the 29th instant.

As attention can only be the true harbinger of success in an undertaking dependent on public estimation for support, he flatters himself that by a uniform endeavour to merit will be to ensure a liberal encouragement. Officers of vessels, Settlers, and all who may have occasion to make his house that of their resort, shall find every accommodation that can be hoped. Dinners will be drest at short notice and sent out if required. Means will be adopted to furnish the labouring orders at a trifling expence.

Was this the first 'take-away' in Australian history?

The couple were also given another hundred acres of land as reward 'for working hard and leading a clean life' and thus became prosperous business and property owners in the fast-blossoming city.

The business obviously flourished to the extent that they could afford to hire additional labour to attend their other family interests. On 6 October 1805, the Sydney Gazette again carried a notice from the Robinsons, on this occasion stating that they:

WANTED

A Shepherd; and also a steady Man to look after a herd of Black Cattle – For further particulars enquire of Rich. John Robinson, Pitts Row.

By 1806, the Robinsons occupied a quarter acre allotment with an orchard and garden in Sydney Town as their 'eating house' continued to thrive. In early 1809 Ann was successful in her application for a liquor licence for the Yorkshire Grey and on 6 September of that year Richard received a hundred-acre land grant in his own name, recorded in the Sydney Gazette of 17 September 1807 as being awarded, 'by the Command of his Honor the Lieutenant Governor'.

New South Wales Governor Gidley King was not to enjoy the same happiness and contentment. He was dogged by ill-health and returned with his family to England in 1807, dying the following year at the age of forty-nine.

It was thus obvious that Richard John Robinson had now emerged from the shadow of his wife and on 21 July 1810 the Yorkshire Grey was issued with a licence in his name to retail beer, ale and porter.

As Sydney town grew, Pitt's Row changed to Pitt Street; it was a main artery in the heart of this now thriving city. The Yorkshire Grey was firmly established at 105 Pitt Street and throughout this time remained under the Robinsons' successful ownership with Richard applying in February 1818 for renewal of the liquor licence granted to him in 1810.

Strangely, just over one year later Richard announced that he intended to leave the Colony and return to England. The Sydney

Gazette of 29 May 1819 records that:

> Richard John Robinson intending to proceed to England
> by the Ship *Surry*, requires Claims to be presented; and
> those indebted to settle their accounts [and the same notice
> further announced that] NB. Mrs Ann Robinson, Wife of the
> Advertiser, remains in the Colony, with full powers to transact
> his Business as though he himself were present.

What was it that prompted this sudden change to both their lives?
After all, they had both been through so much together during their
twenty-seven years of marriage. It was not as though they were still
serving their sentences. Their freedom had been granted some twenty-
five years earlier leaving them free to return had they so wished. On
the other hand perhaps their marriage had run its course – we will
probably never know.

Richard John Robinson was number six on the passenger list of
the 'Surrey' which sailed for England on 23 July 1819 and which did
not arrive in England until December of that year. During this time
Ann was in sole charge of the Yorkshire Grey and in August 1819 she
approached Governor Macquarie for, 'Permission to state unto your
Excellency that some time back I craved your consideration . . . with a
renewal of my lease.' The governor immediately renewed her lease for
another fourteen years, so securing the continuing prosperity of the
Yorkshire Grey.

Whatever the reason for Richard Robinson's return to England, it
seems that during the few months following his departure, Ann must
have had time to think about her life and realised that the separation
was a permanent one. Having secured a renewal of the lease, locals
might have speculated on the advertisement that the gazette carried
on 8 January 1820 for the sale of what had been Richard and Ann's
home and business for the preceding sixteen years. It read:

> To be Sold by Private Contract
> all those extensive and well known Premises, 105 Pitt Street,
> the present Property and Residence of Mrs Anne Robinson,

who is about to leave the Colony by the Ship Admiral
Cockburn. – These Premises are desirably situate for Traders
and Merchants, having a House built of Brick and Stone, a
well-accustomed Butcher' Shop, an extensive Garden well
stocked with Fruit trees, an excellent Well of pure Water, well
supplied at all Seasons; also, an extensive Kitchen and Baker'
Oven – May be viewed and Day, and further Particulars
known by Application on the Premises.

Events had certainly occurred very quickly as the advertisement
appeared hardly one month after her husband would have arrived in
England and certainly before any communication could have been
received from him,

We are therefore left wondering if this had all been planned by
mutual agreement, or whether Ann had taken affairs into her own
hands. As there is no evidence of any subsequent contact between
Ann and Richard back in England Ann seems to have been left with
the proceeds of the sale which could possibly have left her reasonably
well off. This would have depended on their debts at that time.

Within three months Ann had left New South Wales – the Sydney
Gazette of 4 March 1820 reporting her departure on the 'Admiral
Cockburn' as, 'Mrs Robinson of Pitt Street, who has the care of the
two sons of the late Mr T. S. Amos'.

Thomas Sterrop Amos was a London solicitor, a widower who,
with his two young sons, arrived in Sydney in April 1817. He had set
up a practice in the town but died on 9 April 1819. Ann was chaperone
to his two young children, now aged nine and seven years for the
voyage back to England.

According to her baptismal record, Ann was now sixty-six years
of age but according to the transportation records, she was but sixty-
three – however, in any case she had been away from England for
thirty-three years. What would she find on her return?

Her first two children, Thomas Inett and Constance Inett, would
have been forty-two and thirty-nine years old respectively – were
they still alive, and if so, where might they be? And what of her elder
brothers and sister – they had all married prior to Ann's transportation,

but were they still alive in 1820? And what of her two boys by Philip Gidley King – Norfolk now aged thirty-one years and Sydney now thirty-years-old – where had their eventual naval careers taken them since they were despatched from New South Wales at an early age to be educated in England. Ann would have had much to ponder during her voyage home. Now sixty-six, she had left the colony of New South Wales with her life totally transformed – from ignominy and disgrace to wealth and respectability.

The good ship Admiral Cockburn was off Portsmouth on 22 June 1820, just 114 days out of Sydney compared with the 258 days voyage which Ann had endured from Portsmouth to Port Jackson with the First Fleet. Two days later on 24 June the ship was off Gravesend, its voyage completed. What would have been Ann's course of action on disembarking? She would have been heavily burdened with her own personal luggage as well as those of the two Amos boys and, no doubt, would have wanted to get her land-legs after nearly four months at sea.

A contemporary of Ann Inett's.

Her first task would have been to go to the London house or offices of John Amos and present herself and the two Amos boys thereby discharging her responsibilities for the children. But where was she to go then? Where might she live? It is not likely that many people would have known of her arrival back in England. John Amos would have known of his brother's death and most probably have arranged for his nephew's passage with Ann acting as chaperone. It is also quite possible that Norfolk and Sydney knew of her pending arrival. But what about her husband Richard? Had their parting been permanent?

The only other person who might have known would have been the Rev Richard Johnson who had christened both her sons, had officiated at their marriage and who had been Richard Robinson's overseer during the early days in the Colony. Coincidentally, he had now returned and was the incumbent at St Antholin's church in Budge Row Cheapside, less than one mile away from John Amos' office and Norfolk's home in Whitechapel. Any one of these three might have helped Ann and it is reasonable to expect that, with three close connections, she would have received help in finding somewhere to live in that part of London.

Having returned to England, Ann's maternal instincts would no doubt have been aroused for the young children from whom she had been separated some thirty-four years earlier. She would be aching to know what might have become of her children Thomas and Constance, her brothers, sister and the rest of her family circle. So she quite probably returned to Worcestershire – if only to visit. Certainly there are good grounds to believe that she did.

Journeying from London to Worcester would not have been difficult as there were often stage coach services every day between the two cities – and there was always a hostelry offering accommodation at the end of the journey.

Ann would have found Worcester city little changed from how she remembered it some thirty-three years earlier; a mediaeval city of half-timbered buildings lining the narrow streets around the Cathedral and along the eastern banks of the River Severn. The old bridge crossing the river was still standing and the criss-cross roads and streets, even with the more recent houses in the parishes of St John in Bedwardine and its neighbouring St Clement (the other side of the river in those days) would have been substantially the same. The stage coach would have delivered her into the centre of the city, so she might have given a little shiver seeing the Guildhall once again with its horrible memories.

After such a long absence Ann would now find out that her mother had died back in 1791. Her eldest brother John was still living in Rock whilst sister Sarah had been widowed, remarried and was still living in Grimley. Brother William, to whom Ann had seemed particularly close, had possibly taken Constance into his own family following Ann's trial and conviction. However, Ann would have been sad indeed to learn that William had died some four years earlier. William's son James had stood as witness when Constance had married William

Guy, a porter, on 3 August 1809 at St Clements church and in which parish the couple now lived, their address being Turkey Street – now Tybridge Street.

Circumstantial evidence that Ann did actually return to Worcester is that within three months of her arrival at Gravesend she was recognised when the baby daughter of William and Constance Guy was baptised 'Mary Ann Robinson Guy' on 5 September 1820, the child's middle name clearly that of her grandmother just back from the land now referred to as Australia. It also suggests that her daughter was glad to be reunited at last with her natural mother.

So it is comforting to believe that Ann was, in fact, reunited with what was left of her family, and that she was openly and gladly accepted back in their hearts. It is also highly probable that Ann Robinson was re-united – fascinatingly, again in Worcester – with youngest son Sydney from her relationship with Philip Gidley King. Sydney was married at St John in Bedwardine Church Worcester, on 15 March 1825, to local girl Mary Butler, whose family lived in

St John in Bedwardine Church Worcester.

Henwick Road. Interestingly, Sydney gave himself the middle name Inett in signing the marriage register. *Berrow's Worcester Journal* of 17 March 1825, recorded 'Marriage – On Tuesday at St John's by the Rev. B. Dent, Lt. Sydney King RN to Mary, third daughter of the late Mr R. Butler of that place.'

It is a mystery as to what first brought Sydney to Worcester and the circumstances that caused him to meet, then court, Mary Butler. Did his mother actually attend the wedding? Questions that still remain unanswered today. By this time Sydney had enjoyed an illustrious career as a naval officer, having seen active service against the French through the Napoleonic Wars.

Lieutenant Sydney King *c.*1820.

Sydney King's Silver Medal.

There is evidence that he remained in Worcester for a short time after his marriage before being transferred to the Coastguard Service in Whitby where Anne, the first born of the marriage was baptised on 5 January 1826.

Sydney's will proved after his death in 1841 reads:

> In the name of God Amen, I, Sydney King being the natural born son of the later Governor Philip Gidley King, of New South Wales and being christened in the above name and having retained it up to my marriage with my beloved wife, Mary Butler, Spinster, whom I married at St John's Bedwardine near to Worcester and then having taken the name of Inett, my Mother's name, between Sydney and King making my

present name by which I married the most exemplary of wifes . . . Sydney Inett King.

Sydney and his wife Mary went on to have six children, but the family moved around the country with his naval postings and also to Harwich when he was appointed Chief Officer in the Revenue Coastguard. His final appointment was to Southend where, in 1838, he was commended for his role in rescuing personnel from a vessel wrecked off Shoeburyness.

He received the prestigious Silver Medal from 'The Royal National Institute for the Preservation of Life from Shipwreck' – the forerunner of the RNLI – as well as an award from the Royal Humane Society.

Sydney died in Essex in 1841 aged fifty-one, His wife Mary long survived him, dying in London in 1880.

Ann's eldest son Norfolk also pursued an illustrious naval career. In 1807 he was midshipman on HMS *Repulse* operating in the Dardanelles where he distinguished himself during the battles with the Turks. He had been promoted to Lieutenant in 1812 – the first Australasian born officer in the Royal Navy. His first command was the schooner 'Ballahou' in which he served and fought during the Anglo-American War of 1812–14.

He was on the Navy List and drawing a Lieutenant's pay when he married Philadelphia Montague at St James Church Clerkenwell in January 1820. His last known address was Prospect Place Sidney Street Whitechapel. This address has been difficult to tie down as Prospect Place cannot be found on any maps of that time. Sidney Street, off Whitechapel Road, however, is well chronicled.

It is disappointing that so much of Ann's life following her return to England is based on circumstantial evidence, but that wealth of evidence is such that the probability of it being true is reasonably high.

So where did Ann actually end up? We have a burial record for an Ann Robinson who died on 27 November in Stepney, her last address being registered as Blue Anchor Yard close to the Royal Mint and not far from the Tower of London. The age given at death was sixty-nine years, which would be right for our Ann. More importantly this

BURIALS in the Parish of					BURIALS in the Parish of *Mary Whitechapel*				
in the County of			In the Year 18 27		in the County of *Middlesex*			in the Year 1827	
Name	Abode	When Buried	Age	By whom the Ceremony was performed	Name	Abode	When Buried	Age	By whom the Ceremony was performed
Cath. Murphy	Essex St	November 25	40	J. Matthews &c.	Marg... Knight	Rosemary Lane	November 30	1	J. Mathias &c.
Mary Matthews	B. Anchor Yd	25	20	do	Sophia Silwood	do	30	2	do
John Driscoll	John St	25	60	do	Mary Clayton	do	30	40	do
Ann Robinson	B. Anchor Yd	27	69	do	Charlotte Hardy	Ditch Lane	December 2	52	do
Joseph Dira	Charlott St	27	59	do	P... Strahan	2 Ann St	2	30	do
Sarah Parker	High St	24	39	do	James Sandys	Guiston St	2	2	do
Joseph Ludlow	Angel Alley	24	31	do	Jeremiah Sullivan	Skinny St Georges St	2	12	do
Martha Collier	Wentworth maze	30	70	do	Mary Ralph	Guisha ...	2	11	do

Ann	Robinson	B. Anchor Yd	27	69	do
No.					

St Mary's burial record (above).
Ann's entry (enlarged below).

was situated almost equidistant to the offices of John Amos, her son
Norfolk's home in Whitechapel and the Revd Johnson's church in
Cheapside.

Some doubt has been expressed concerning the merits of Ann's
address being 8 Anchor Yard or whether she lived at Blue Anchor
Yard. This is due to the interpretation put on the handwriting in the
official records as the first figure could be read either as a figure eight
or the capital letter 'b', as an abbreviation for 'blue'. It is significant
that Blue Anchor Yard was within the same area administered by
St Mary's Church where Ann Robinson was buried, and the record
seems to appear more as the letter 'b' than the number eight. Whilst

some need more concrete proof, the probability is that this is, in fact, Ann Inett/Robinson's burial record. Unfortunately all evidence of a grave was destroyed when the church was devastated in a bombing raid during WWII.

Ann's son Norfolk's address was certainly Prospect Place Sidney Street Whitechapel. This address has been difficult to tie down as Prospect Place cannot be found on any maps of that time. It was possibly a small courtyard within a larger building in Sidney Street, off Whitechapel Road, a road that is well chronicled for other reasons.

Whitechapel is currently perceived to have been a place that one chose not to go to in the nineteenth century. The road itself was not particularly squalid through most of this period – it was the

St Mary's, Whitechapel.

warrens of small dark streets branching from it that contained the greatest suffering, filth and danger. It was filled to bursting with all types of immigrants by the nineteenth century, and the place eventually became known for prostitution. It would later become infamous as the hunting ground of Jack the Ripper, also for the siege of Sidney street. So why would a distinguished naval officer live in such an area?

Local historian and author Derek Morris explains that in those days it was not uncommon to find social classes at opposite ends of the spectrum to be living on the same street. In any case, it was close to the docks and therefore most appropriate for a naval man. Norfolk King apparently remained there for the rest of his life dying, in 1839, aged fifty.

As for Governor Philip Gidley King, the father of Ann's two boys, he had returned to England in November 1807. The family home was in Tooting, a village to the south west of London, where he lived with his wife Anna Josepha who had brought Ann's two boys up during the early years of their lives.

Philip Gidley King died at an address in Norton Street (now disappeared) London on 3 September 1808 and was buried at St Nicholas

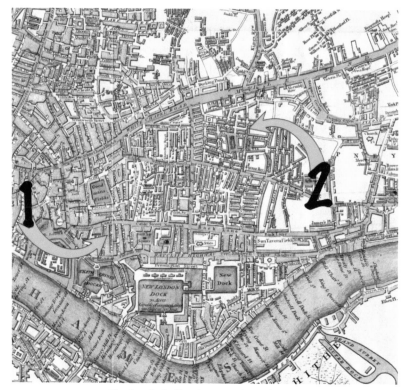

The East End of London around 1825 showing
Blue Anchor Yard (1) and Sidney Street (2) where Norfolk lived.

St Nicholas Church Tooting.

Church Tooting six days later. It is not known if Ann was aware of this event or if she ever visited the grave.

Many years later, Gidley King's widow joined their natural son Philip who had retired back to New South Wales. She remained there until her death in 1844. In 1988 the descendants of the Kings arranged for the tombstone of her husband Philip Gidley King to be taken from the graveyard of St Nicholas Church and brought to Australia where it was placed in an enclosure next to Anna Josepha's grave.

XI
EPILOGUE

So began the colonisation and population of the new continent that would come to be called Australia by the explorer Matthew Flinders who referred to it in his book *A Voyage to Terra Australis* around 1814. This policy of transportation of convicts to this land would continue for another eighty-three years.

And what about the *Lady Penrhyn*? Having sailed from New South Wales to China (her prime purpose), she was sold and placed on a regular run to Jamaica. Then, on 22 July 1811, she was taken by the French privateer Duke of Danzig while on passage from London to Grenada She then suffered the fate of so many ships at the hands of pirates by being set on fire then scuttled.

How many of Australians today can trace their roots back to those eight women who were sent there via the cells and courtroom of the Guildhall Worcester? There are indeed many who avidly research their family background in order to find some connection with these early settlers. Which is amusing in a way as it is natural for one to feel embarrassed if a member of one's family turns to criminality. On the other hand, time is a great healer and curiosity takes over. Then pride. Pride that one's ancestor was part of the founding of a great nation.

Certainly there are quite a few of Olivia Gascoigne/Lucas's descendants around. Some time ago, James Donohoe sent me the list below showing the currently known numbers of descendants of Olivia and Nathaniel Lucas, noting also that it is possible that we are already into the eleventh generation, since some of the tenth generation would now be in their twenties.

First generation: 13 children
Second generation: 120 grandchildren
Third generation: 703 great-grandchildren
Fourth generation: 2,303 first-great-grandchildren
Fifth generation: 4,792 second-great-grandchildren
Sixth generation: 8,933 third-great-grandchildren
Seventh generation: 14,918 fourth-great-grandchildren
Eighth generation: 9,780 fifth-great-grandchildren
Ninth generation: 1,075 sixth-great-grandchildren
Tenth generation: 27 seventh-great-grandchildren

That is an extraordinary total of more than 42,660 direct descendants. He adds that his current best estimate is that around 34,978 of those descendants could well be living today. Astonishing!

History keeps reminding us that the convicts were all of the criminal class, the nation's 'dregs'. If that were true, why were there aristocrats and middle-class people among those sent out? Why the very high proportion of trades people and the skilled?

Researching the list of one hundred and ninety-four female convicts on that First Fleet, I couldn't help thinking that there was something odd about their places of origin. One hundred and fifty-two came from London which is to be expected as that was where the greatest accumulation of criminals was to be found. I would then have expected the next largest numbers to come from the other main cities and ports due to the higher incidences of crime in those areas. However, that was not the case.

Surprisingly, our eight women made Worcester the next largest contingent from the whole of England. Followed by Shrewsbury with just four and Gloucester and Southwark offering just three each. Then two each from Thetford and Maidstone – all of those conurbations being medium to small provincial towns.

What I found difficult to understand was why there should only be one convict sent from fifteen larger towns such as: Liverpool, Newcastle, Durham, Derby, Reading, Winchester, York and Lincoln etc. where there would have been many more criminals simply because of their greater population.

Is it possible that there was some kind of purpose in the selection of convicts for this venture? London was a renowned centre of crime, debauchery and general iniquity. Would it really be feasible for such a venture to succeed with all the convicts coming from such a place? Of course not.

Whilst our own eight women were all convicts, their lives to date would have been relatively, if not completely, free from such depravity. As opposed to the prostitutes and thieves from the big city, they would possess many of the skills required in setting up a new community. Many of them, having come from the provinces, would have experience of farming, keeping house and other domestic skills that would prove vital in the years to come.

Contrary to popular belief, Australia (as America before) was not just a repository for thieves, rogues, murderers and the dregs of society. In fact it was relatively common for upright citizens to suffer deportation simply because they upset the establishment or their well appointed employer.

For instance, many years after our main story, the Tolpuddle Martyrs: George Loveless, James Loveless, Thomas Standfield, John Standfield, James Hammet and James Brine, six men from the Village of Tolpuddle in England were transported to New South Wales in 1834 simply for trying to form a trades union. Today they could easily be applauded for standing up for their principles.

Then there were the Scottish Martyrs, five men who promoted the ideals of the French Revolution: liberty, equality and fraternity. For promoting these views they too were transported to Australia.

Even aristocrats from England's establishment fell foul of the law in those days. These included: James Hardy Vaux – an eccentric who, despite acknowledging the folly of his ways, found it impossible to resist the temptation to break the law; Francis Greenway, a short-fused architect who made too many enemies simply by rubbing people the wrong way; James Grant, who discharged a weapon in a gentleman's 'duel' after his honour had been tainted; Sir Henry Brown Hayes, a knight and sheriff of Cork who kidnapped a lady and forced her to marry him.

Their often innocent servants could be at risk too. In a house of nobility, if an item went missing or was misplaced, the servant

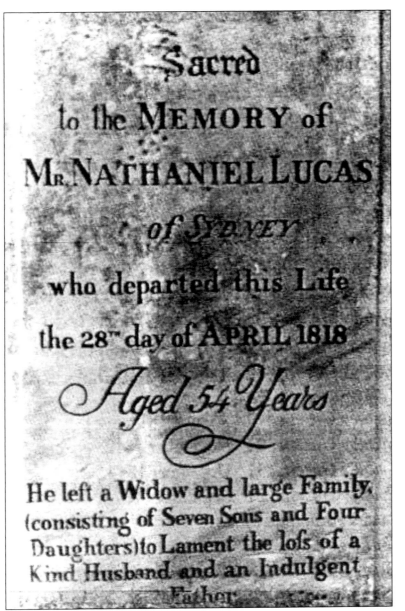

Nathaniel's original gravestone, now in the porch of St Luke's,
Liverpool, New South Wales which was his last building contract.

was often blamed resulting in catastrophic circumstances for the 'accused'. Other servants formed relationships with their masters and risked being accused of theft when the master wanted the relationship to end.

On another level, more unscrupulous persons might well have found it convenient to make a false accusation of theft to cover up a loss due to their own failings, maybe to turn the blame on to others in order to cover up their own crime, or to contrive the grant of a reward for helping to gain a conviction. Convictions were invariably assured even when there was a lack of evidence because the accuser would normally be from a higher social level and their word therefore carried more weight..

Of course there were gangsters and prostitutes amongst the deportees. There was a role for them. Somebody had to do the labouring and the entertaining! The generalisation though is wrong. It is fair to assert now that the British, in the main, sent the cream of the English convicts in order for the colony to succeed.

There are now too many First Fleet descendants who have found enough records on their ancestors to recreate a profile about them which reveals their forebears to have been solid citizens and fine examples of parents once away from the desperate life they were forced to live in England.

Most were truly nation builders. Their children in the main were good people too. The Botany Bay exercise was meant to work. The 'dregs' of society alone would not have made things happen.

These pioneers founded the modern Australian family and the nation that it has become. The material coming from family researchers is showing up more and more fallacies about the interpretation of the nation's recorded origins.

Olivia's grave (with many others) was obliterated when the old Cypress Street cemetery in Launceston (Tasmania) was bulldozed to make way for school playing fields. The photo above shows the vicinity of her resting place (somewhat ironically back behind bars). The plaque below marks the site on Norfolk Island where Lieutenant Gidley King first landed to form the new colony there.

A plaque sited at Emily Bay Norfolk Island commemorating the original settlers.

A monument in Brighton-Le-Sands, Botany Bay in New South Wales
commemorating the landing of the First Fleet.
The monument has the names of most of those who arrived on the First Fleet.

XII
COINCIDENCES

The first concerns the *Lady Penrhyn* and how it got its name. It appears that the two owners of this new vessel, William Cropton Server who would captain the ship on its first voyage, and William 'BIlly Biscuit' Curtis a past lord mayor of London whose company manufactured sea biscuits, are both believed to have been business acquaintances of one Richard Pennant, the first Baron of Penrhyn. He was certainly very wealthy, owning a number of plantations in Jamaica and had served as member of Parliament for Petersfield and later, Liverpool. It is through this association that the ship became named in honour of the Baron's wife.

The coincidence is that the Right Honourable the Lord Penrhyn, the current and seventh Baron Simon Douglas-Pennant lives in Castlemorton, Malvern, just a few miles from Worcester.

Then, for some unaccountable reason, I found myself drawn to the story of these eight women. I could never figure out why – until much later . . . Just as an amusing aside, during my research of these first settlers I came across the following coincidences:

Ann and her husband lived for a time in Parramatta and later moved to Burwood – *my second home was in Parramatta before I moved to Burwood with my job.*

Ann and her husband owned the Yorkshire Grey Hotel in Sydney – *the Yorkshire Grey near Worcester is one of my favourite restaurants.*

Ann and her husband owned an extensive plot of land at Pitt's Row in Sydney – *I have probably trodden on that ground, possibly daily, as I worked in Pitt Street (as it is now called) in Sydney for several years.*

St John-in-Bedwardine church saw the marriage of Ann's youngest son Sydney, at which Ann is believed to have been present – *my youngest son was married at that same altar.*

Philip Gidley King's widow Anna Josepha, who had brought up Norfolk and Sydney during the early years of their lives, lived in Tooting (southwest London) – *I was born and lived in Tooting until I emigrated to Australia in 1966.*

Ann Robinson/Inett is understood to have been at her grandchild's christening at St Clement's Church, Worcester – *my grandson went to St Clements Primary School.*

As Chairman of Licensing I have chaired a great number of quasi-judicial hearings – *in that very same courtroom where Ann was sentenced.*

And finally, whilst researching the early free colonisation of Australia, I came across this picture of David and Alexina Duncan (below). Whilst there were thousands of free settlers in Australia (there was one with the very First Fleet of convicts in 1788), David and Alexina were on the very first ship of 'assisted' free settlers, known as 'Bounty Immigrants'.

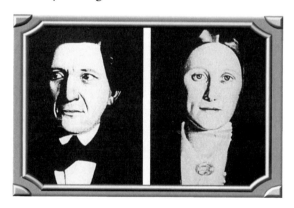

They arrived in Port Phillip on 27 October 1839 on the first assisted settlers ship called, the *David Clark.*

How strange is that?

XIII
LOOSE ENDS AND OLIVIA GASCOIGNE

The story you have just read is my way of using the known facts in an attempt to bring to life the extraordinary experiences of these eight women. There are, however, a few loose ends that prevent me from finishing this story to my own satisfaction.

One mystery is that of Mary Abel's married name of Tilley. She is recorded in *Berrow's Worcester Journal* at her trial as Mary Tilley alias Abell (a misspelling) and in various other places as just Mary Abel. Was it a coincidence that she later married a man with the same name? A Smith marrying a Smith, or two Jones getting together might be unremarkable but two Tilleys?

Another issue that would have been fulfilling to resolve would have been to discover what happened to John Robinson after he returned to England. This might have given clues as to why he and Ann went their separate ways, seemingly never meeting or even contacting each other again.

Then Ann, who clearly had contact with both sons by Gidley King on her return to England – but did she ever communicate with Gidley King again? Probably not given the difference in their social standing, but she might well have known of the death of the father of her children. So did she ever visit his grave in Tooting which was just only seven miles from her home near the Tower of London?

On a personal note, as I lived in Tooting for the first twenty years of my life, I would very much like to know where Gidley King was living when he died.

However, the most significant loose end that has caused me real problems in being able to look back on my book with satisfaction concerns the early years in Olivia Gascoigne's life. Unlike the other women, who all came from similar poor backgrounds, Olivia might be different. I must emphasise at this point that at the moment of writing, absolutely nothing is known about her family background so I have to assume that she was simply a typical young woman who committed a crime and suffered the consequences with her compatriots.

That was not the case when I started writing this story. Part of the intrigue was that Olivia was thought to have been from an aristocratic background which made her exceedingly interesting and certainly would have given the story an edge.

Many descendants in Australia hold firm beliefs in Olivia's highly connected ancestry of which there are several seemingly plausible theories. They are, however, all held together by numerous coincidences some which seem to stretch the imagination almost to breaking point – but no matter how strange or far-fetched they might be, some cannot be disproved. I therefore have to remember that the truth can sometimes be stranger than fiction.

For that reason I have included this last section to recognise the controversy of Olivia's parentage which would make an interesting book in its own right.

Before I go through some of the more interesting avenues concerning Olivia's possible antecedents I firmly believe that if Olivia was from aristocratic stock, then some kind of evidence should have been found by now. Families such as these were mostly well educated and their family records should have thrown up some kind of evidence, even of rumours, by now. The fact that nothing whatsoever exists, could be seen as circumstantial evidence that she was nothing more than a poor unfortunate woman of the time.

To begin with, just the name 'Gascoigne' seems, at first, out of place and not one given to the average working class family, certainly not for a lowly servant. Surprisingly, this name was not as rare as one might have thought. The name (with its derivatives Gaskins Gasken etc.) was much more common in the north of the county where it bordered on the outer Birmingham townships and hamlets.

Many theories offered on the internet centred around an aristocratic upbringing. This possibility was fuelled when an archivist (unnamed) at the Worcestershire Records Office pointed out that one of their First Fleeters on the *Lady Penrhyn* was recorded in gaol records as 'highly connected'. The name was not then recalled by the informant but Olivia was the only one of the eight concerned who might have fitted this postulation because of her name and also because she had received the Royal Prerogative:

> Whereas Olive Gascoigne was severally attainted at this assizes of the severe felony of stealing the value of above 40 shillings in a dwelling house, His Majesty hath been graciously pleased to extend Royal Mercy to her on the condition of her being severally transported beyond the seas for and during the term of 7 years. It is thereby ordered by this Court that the prisoner Olive Gascoigne be transported beyond the seas accordingly as soon as conveniently may be pursuant to the acts of Parliament in this case made provided that Reginald Lygon and Charles Trubshaw Withers Esquires, two of His Majesty's Justices of the Peace for the county of Worcester, do contract with any person or persons for the performance of the transportation and order such and the like sufficient security to be taken as the same acts of Parliament direct. I also cause the prisoner Olive Gascoigne pursuant to such contract or contracts to be delivered over by the gaoler of the county of Worcester (in whose custody she now is) to the person or persons contracting for him or to his or their assizes and certify such contract or contracts and security to be taken at the next assizes. General Gaol delivery to be holden for the county of Worcester in order to have the prisoner be certified and contract or contracts and security filed among the records of this court.
>
> By the Court.

It seemed strange at first that this Royal Mercy was not granted until 28 December 1788, just over nine months after her sentence, but that would have been due simply to the time court administration and communications took in those days.

Could it have been that receipt of such a document might be used by a family conscious of their position, wishing to invoke the personal intervention of the Monarch on their daughter's behalf in order to mitigate the shame she had brought on the family? A nice thought, but not borne out by the facts. The Royal Prerogative document was, in fact, an administrative consequence of the judge commuting the death sentence and would have been issued for any such event to whomsoever it applied.

In any case, the record above shows that it was the presiding judge His Honour George Nares, who was retiring, who requested His Majesty's clemency to commute the sentence as his final act from the bench.

The first theory to suggest this possible aristocratic background was that Olivia was the daughter of John Gascoigne the High Sheriff of Yorkshire whose family home was the largest castle in England, Wentworth Castle and Sarah Vernon of Hanbury Hall. Through that connection Olivia would have been related to D'Arcy Wentworth who had a distinguished career in the Australian colonies and whose son William Wentworth was the famous explorer and politician. This connection made her a cousin of the Campbells of Ashfield, thereby providing a link to the Dukes of Argyle and thence to the dukes of Clarence and Cumberland through legitimate and clandestine associations.

These connections were deemed important evidence in confirming her heritage with the added evidence of streets near Olivia's dwelling in Sydney which had been given the names Argyle, Clarence and Cumberland. More relevant would be the truth that place names were actually named after those with high connections in government or patronage – not because of some vague connection to a mere convict.

You might think that the daughter of such noble and privileged birth could never find herself ending up in the British courts and ultimately sentenced to hang for her crime, but you would be wrong. Much has been written about daughters of upper class families who rebelled against being paraded on the marriage market in order to be judged by eligible suitors on their excellent needlework, genteel manners and the size of their dowries. Others who felt so stifled were known to have left the tentacles of the family to seek a more exciting life.

However, in checking this theory I found that there never was a John Gascoigne in the position of high sheriff, and the incumbent when Olivia was born was in fact Sir Thomas Wentworth. Then a colleague of mine, who is an authority on the Vernons, confirmed that such a liaison with Sarah never existed. So that whole theory was a complete red herring.

Another interesting theory, and one that possibly held more credit was that Olivia was a member of the family of the Baron Lasingcroft Parlington – Sir Thomas Gascoigne. It is thought she may have been one of his two illegitimate children from an affair with a French Tutor during his youth. Sir Thomas' grandfather, when widowed, became a Monk of the Benedictines whilst his aunt was the mother abbess of the Poor Clares The reason for this particular avenue of thought is due to the coincidence of their names and that Olivia's crime was committed in Severn Stoke, just a mile or so from Hanley Castle, the headquarters of the Benedictine Order of Monks and Poor Clare Order of Nuns. At the time of her arrest, Sir Thomas was standing for Parliament and it is suspected by some that Olivia was framed in order to hide any possible embarrassment at his daughter's illegitimacy. But again, not one shred of evidence to support this theory.

In spending countless hours searching local parish and land and tythe records, I followed up another possibility that Olivia could have been the granddaughter of a John Gaskins (a derivative or misspelling of Gascoigne) and Olive Partridge who married at St Andrews Church Droitwich in 1724. For me this was a much more likely possibility as there was the coincidence of surname strengthened by the similarity of first name on the female side which was commonly passed down through the family in those days. However, records for the ensuing years are sketchy due to missing documents and others illegible due to age and damage. Therefore this remains as nothing more than a remote possibility.

In conclusion, the only way that this mystery can come to any satisfactory conclusion would be to compare DNA samples from known descendants of the families in question.

On the other hand, there is the distinct possibility that Olivia's husband Nathaniel Lucas might well have had wealthy connections in his family of which he was probably blissfully unaware. Some time after Nathaniel's death a John Lucas, first cousin of Nathaniel's father, died. He had been an investor in both the first and second South Seas Company's and had become quite wealthy. In his will of 1797, he left his considerable estate to his cousins including Nathaniel's father.

I, for one, would have been more than happy to be able to prove Olivia to be highly connected. It would elevate this story out of all proportion. The enormous numbers of her descendants would really have something to talk about; there would be a best seller book and then a film – fantastic. Even Worcester and the fabulous Guildhall would have something to rival Coventry's Lady Godiva and Stratford's Ann Hathaway.

The fact for the time being is that Olivia remains a poor servant who committed theft, was convicted and sentenced to death, then transported to the new land 'Beyond the Seas', who became a respected person in her own right and who was to become the progeny for the largest ancestral tree that exists in Australia today.

Good on her!

ACKNOWLEDGEMENTS
AND OTHER SOURCES

Mike Grundy for his articles on Ann Inett and who fired my initial interest.

Peter Mackay and Helen Styles in particular, for their considered and evidentially supported research which helped me greatly in keeping to established facts

Edward Inett's articles in *The Rock* and his extensively researched family history in *Inett – What's in a Name.*

Dr Ron Inett, descendant and family historian.

Simon Douglas-Pennant, Lord Penrhyn the seventh baron, who provided an insight into the naming of the *Lady Penrhyn.*

Derek Morris an established authority and author who provided a realistic insight into Whitechapel in the late eighteenth century.

Janet Hathaway of Bell End Farm who very kindly allowed me into her home where I experienced Sarah Bellamy's one-time workplace and saw the main fireplace that Sarah no doubt tended so many times.

Trevor and Judi Lagstrom for sharing a copy of their book *Prisoners in Paradise.*

James Donohue for his insights into the various theories of Olivia's parentage.

Glenda Miskelly and Ken McCubbin for their extensive writings, comments and communications which all contributed to my research.

Carpenter, Jeff *Worcester's Guildhall – An Historical Guide.*
Fidlon and Ryan, (editors) *The Journal of Arthur Bowes Smyth: Surgeon, Lady Penrhyn 1787–1789.*
Gillen, Mollie *The Founders of Australia.*

Yarwood, A. T. *Growing up in the First Fleet.*

Belbroughton Historical Society.
Berrow's Worcester Journal archives.
National Library of Australia information desk.
Worcester History Centre.
Worcester News.
Worcester City Council.
Worcestershire County Council archives.

I also have to acknowledge the enormous number of websites available
such as:
www.members.iinet.net.au/~perthdps/convicts/1stfleet.html
www.australianhistoryresearch.info/the-first-fleet
www.gutenberg.net.au/first-fleet.html
www.firstfleetfellowship.org.au